# SEA TURTLES TO SIDEWINDERS

# SEA TURTLES TO SIDEWINDERS

## A GUIDE TO THE MOST FASCINATING **REPTILES & AMPHIBIANS** OF THE **WEST**

**CHARLES HOOD, ERIN WESTEEN,** and
**JOSÉ GABRIEL MARTÍNEZ-FONSECA**

**Timber Press | Portland, Oregon**

Photo credits appear on page 238.

Published in 2021 by Timber Press, Inc.
The Haseltine Building
133 S.W. Second Avenue, Suite 450
Portland, Oregon 97204-3527
timberpress.com

Printed in China

Text and cover design by Sarah Crumb

ISBN 978-1-64326-035-8

A catalog record for this book is available from the Library of Congress.

# CONTENTS



page 123

## AMPHIBIANS



## REPTILES

page 70

page 217

page 118

# INTRODUCTION

This is a book that will help you appreciate and celebrate the amazing diversity of reptiles and amphibians of western North America. Using this book, you will be able to identify the things you see and know where to look for more interesting animals. ▶

[above] This book's eastern range border is the Continental Divide, where rain and snow split into separate flows. On one side, water drains to the Pacific, and on the other, into the Atlantic.

[previous page] Horned lizards look like tanks; one defense is squirting blood from their eyes.

We use the Continental Divide as our eastern boundary; this is the watershed that follows the mountains and splits runoff into two directions. West of the Continental Divide, water flows into the Pacific, and on the east, the Atlantic, with the self-contained Great Basin (which drains into itself) in the middle. We use Canada and Mexico as the north and south boundaries. That means we are interested in species that occur in Arizona, California, Nevada, Oregon, Utah, and Washington, plus the western parts of Montana, Wyoming, Colorado, and New Mexico.

Herpetologists are professional scientists who study reptiles and amphibians, and the animals they specialize in are collectively known as herps. Non-professionals who like these animals are called herpers, and when they set out to look for wild frogs and turtles and snakes and lizards, they are going herping. Some herpers have permits to capture wild animals; this book is about the "watch, don't touch" side of herping—we encourage you to identify as many species as you can but urge you to leave all the herps you come across alone.

The formal term *herpetology* (from the Greek, "crawling on the ground") has been around since the 1820s. To go more deeply into this subject, see the helpful resources in the appendix, and please contact any of the authors if you want to know more about how to enter the exciting field of herpetology.

## What is a reptile?

By reptiles, we mean a large group that includes turtles, lizards, and snakes. Reptiles breathe air, lay eggs, have scales, and are cold-blooded (ectothermic), which means they use external sources like sunlight or warm rocks to maintain suitable body temperatures. This group also contains the worm lizards, the tuatara of New Zealand (which looks a lot like a lizard but isn't), and the crocodilians. Crocodilians are more closely related to birds than they are to other reptiles. This may seem counterintuitive, but birds and crocodiles (and their relatives) have a lot in common, including the type of parental care they give to their offspring. In this book we won't focus on these other animals because they don't occur naturally in western North America, although sometimes a pet caiman or crocodile turns up in a marsh.

Crocodilians like this baby spectacled caiman are more closely related to birds than to lizards and snakes.

Many people consider reptiles to be "slimy," but they are not. Reptiles are *scaly*, not slimy.

For technical reasons, on paper all living birds are also reptiles; to avoid confusion, we will use the layperson's definition of reptile and exclude birds.

Let's take a tour of the primary reptile categories.

**Turtles ~350 species worldwide**

Animals in this group are easily recognizable by the fact that they carry their houses around with them in the form of the shell, or carapace. The turtle's shell is a special adaptation derived from their ribs. That means that turtles don't have ribs within their shell, as one might imagine—the shell *is* their ribs. And since the shell is rigid, that means turtles don't breathe the way other animals do, by expanding and contracting muscles attached to the ribcage. Though turtles are primarily aquatic, they must come up to the surface to breathe, and they do so via special mechanisms, including moving their necks and limbs to expand their lungs. Some turtles can actually breathe through their butts—okay, not really their butts, but their cloaca, the organ through which all herps excrete waste and reproduce. This is mostly needed during hibernation, to ensure that oxygen from the water can be absorbed by the blood.

The nesting behavior of some turtles, especially sea turtles, is dramatic, with many females laying eggs in the same location. Some turtles have what is known as temperature-dependent sex determination. Basically, if the temperature goes over a certain threshold, all the eggs will develop as one sex (usually females at high temperatures, but not always). As climate change worsens, turtles are especially at risk. If all the eggs develop as one sex, mating opportunities will decrease, potentially leading to serious population declines. For more about this, see pages 22–27.

What is the difference between a tortoise and a turtle? Just as all squares are rectangles, all tortoises are turtles. Tortoises are special turtles that live on land all the time, instead of spending all or part of their time in water. Some of the best-known turtles are the giant tortoises of Galapagos, which can live to be 188 years old (and perhaps more than that).

### Lizards ~7,000 species worldwide

Both lizards and snakes belong to a group of animals known as lepidosaurs; some key characteristics of this group include shedding their skin, losing their tails (most species), and males having paired copulatory organs (hemipenes). Tail dropping is generally considered an adaptation to distract predators. Imagine you are chasing a tasty-looking lizard and suddenly its tail pops off and starts wriggling around in front of you. While you are distracted, the lizard makes a dashing escape. The tail will grow back in a few weeks. Some other cool defensive adaptations in lizards include cryptic color (spiny lizards, 161), intense bursts of sprinting speed (sand lizards, 144), spurting blood from their eyes (horned lizards, 149), and mouths full of venom (Gila monster, 111).

Lizards can be small (a few inches long in some geckos and chameleons) or massive (10-foot Komodo dragon). Some are cryptic; others are brightly colored. Many are excellent climbers (anoles); others are adept swimmers (marine iguanas). With so many species, lizards encompass nearly every imaginable niche. Luckily, we have lots of lizard species in the American West, and we will discuss them in depth in the species accounts. Most are out in daytime, and many can be found in all the places people like to go, from trails in the Grand Canyon to backyards to rest stops along I-10. If we were giving out awards for the most fun, accessible reptile group, lizards would get first prize.

### Snakes ~3,500 species worldwide

Snakes are just special lizards . . . lizards that happen to lack legs. Though there are many legless lizards (lizards that have lost forelimbs, hindlimbs, or both—see page 115), snakes are unique. Snakes basically use only one of the lungs in their elongated bodies, with the second reduced to vestigial size; they have many jaw bones connected

This stunning eyelash viper is one of the approximately 3,500 snake species worldwide.

by soft tissue, which allows them to eat large prey; and they lack eyelids and external ears. The flickering, forked tongue has a simple explanation. In zipping its tongue in and out, a snake (and a few other species, like the Gila monster) samples the air. Odors in the air exist in really minute particles. The flicking allows the snake to "taste" those, processing the particles with its Jacobson's organ, which is located inside the roof of the mouth. They then can "see" the world around them, a bit like a bat or dolphin using echolocation.

Snakes vary in size from the large pythons and anacondas, which go past 25 feet, to the 4-inch-long threadsnake of the Caribbean, which looks more like a worm than a snake (see page 176 for our native threadsnakes). Although venomous species, like rattlesnakes, give all snakes a bad rap, less than 20% of snakes possess venom that is actually harmful to humans. Greater risk to ecology comes from the introduction of non-native snakes; many people are familiar with the plague of Burmese pythons which has wiped out so many mammals in the Everglades.

# What is an amphibian?

The word *amphibian* translates roughly to "both lives," which refers to the ability of these animals—frogs, salamanders, and caecilians, a type of legless animal—to live in water and on land. We will focus on frogs and salamanders as our American representatives of this worldwide group. Amphibians possess the unique ability to breathe through their skin in addition to their lungs. They require moisture to keep their skin wet enough to absorb oxygen—they will desiccate and die in overly arid environments. Most amphibians are nocturnal for this reason, and the best time to find amphibians is at night.

## Frogs ~7,000 species worldwide

Frogs occur nearly everywhere, with the exception of the North and South Poles. They are generally good jumpers—thanks to their long and powerful hind legs—but frog species have adapted to a variety of lifestyles, including burrowing types, climbing types, and aquatic types.

Frogs lay eggs in or near water. Because to many predators frog eggs make a tasty snack, frogs have evolved elaborate parental care strategies, including carrying eggs and babies around, swallowing (but not eating) eggs so that they can hatch safely in mom's stomach, and laying eggs over water. Eggs develop into tadpoles, then froglets, and finally into adult frogs.

One aspect of frog ecology familiar to many is their habit of calling, usually after dark and in spring, though you can hear them year-round. Using their large vocal sacs, male frogs call earnestly in hopes of attracting a mate. Early spring after a heavy rain is often a good time to search for frogs—just follow the calls. Bats in the tropical rainforest know this trick too, and one species is even called the frog-eating bat. Sometimes it works the other

way around: the cane toad, a species that can reach 9 inches across, has been recorded eating bats.

Frogs are amphibians; this glass frog (with a mass of eggs) lives in trees in the tropics.

Poison dart frogs (aka poison arrow frogs) are small and vivid, and can make any rainforest hike in Costa Rica a special treat. The bright colors are used to warn potential predators about toxins, many of which are sequestered from the frogs' diets. Some are so poisonous that they were used by Indigenous peoples of Colombia to coat the tips of their weapons. No poison dart frogs occur north of Central America, but they are popular in the pet trade.

A toad is just a bumpy kind of frog. Toads differ from frogs in that they usually live in less water-centric habitat and usually lay a differently shaped chain of eggs, and some species are adapted to long periods waiting underground in between rainy seasons. You already know this, but we want to say it again: neither toads nor frogs (nor any animal in this book) can give you warts.

### Salamanders ~700 species worldwide

Salamanders are perhaps the most secretive of our herps; most are nocturnal and prefer to live underneath damp rocks or logs. However, we here in North America are very lucky, as global salamander diversity peaks here. Salamanders are characterized by elongated bodies, blunt snouts, short and often stocky limbs, and large eyes. They are not lizards; the two lineages haven't shared a common ancestor for about 350 million years—since before the dinosaurs.

Salamanders start out as eggs, most of which are laid in water. When they morph into larvae, they possess gills (like fish). Eventually, many will leave the water and morph into terrestrial adults. But some adult salamanders (such as the axolotl, a popular pet) retain the juvenile form.

Though the general body plan is consistent across most salamanders, they vary quite a bit in length, and one group in Asia, the well-named giant salamanders, can reach 6 feet (though 3 feet is more common). They also vary ecologically. Some species are highly specialized to live in caves and can no longer see; others are excellent climbers and live high in the rainforest canopy. Most salamanders are generalist feeders, enjoying meals of worms, snails, slugs, and bugs.

Some salamanders, like the California newt, possess a poison called tetrodotoxin, which exudes from their skin. It is strong enough to kill most vertebrates, including many of their predators, if they ingest it. You should never handle an animal that you cannot positively ID, and you should be especially careful with newts (page 49). Luckily, newts advertise their toxicity with bright orange coloration.

## What is a species?

Though this question may seem harmless, taking sides on the species question has been the subject of hot debate in the biological world for many years. We use the biological species concept: a species is a group of organisms that successfully interbreeds, or can successfully interbreed, in nature.

What does it mean for individuals to have the ability to interbreed? Imagine a large population of frogs, living happily in the desert. Suddenly, a huge highway is constructed in between them, creating two smaller populations, so they are no longer able to reach each other. Yet technically they could still mate if the highway was not there. Under our definition, they will be considered the same species, because they could (for the moment) still interbreed, except that they simply cannot reach one another.

Note that this definition does not say anything about an animal's physical appearance. Some animals may look similar but do not interbreed (some of the spiny lizards or slender salamanders, for example), while others may look completely different and still be members of the same species, such as the various morphs of rosy boa.

Subspecies exist only in context of a reference species. Consider again our frogs. If, after many years, the two populations on either side of the highway begin to adapt or change such that they become discrete entities, they may be considered subspecies. A species can be divided into two or more subspecies, but a single subspecies cannot be recognized in isolation without a reference species.

As you can see, the issue of species vs. subspecies is a tricky one with lots of gray areas. It is best to consider speciation as a continuum with many stages, rather than as a binary distinction between one species and another. Often, subspecies will be assigned for practical management reasons. For example, if a particular population is (a) isolated from other populations of the same species and (b) at risk of population decline from a variety of reasons (habitat degradation, climate change, invasive species, etc.), it may make sense to designate this group of animals as a distinct subspecies so that it may receive protection under the law.

In that case, the scientific name of the subspecies is given as a third element, so one can easily recognize, for example, that *Sceloporus occidentalis taylori* is a subspecies of *S. occidentalis*. Sometimes the subspecies gets its own common name, too—in this example, Sierra fence lizard.

Morphs are individuals of the same species that appear distinct to the eye, like the differently patterned corn snakes or ball pythons. Morphs are very popular in the pet trade: by breeding individuals with desired colors and/or patterns, breeders can produce more offspring with that same look. Some breeding pairs may produce offspring with some elements that resemble one parent and others taken from the other parent—the pastel ball python morph has light coloration (like the albino morph) but maintains the patterning of the wild type. The variety of morphs is a function of how heritable different elements of color and pattern are. Crossbreeding is beyond the scope of this book, but go to any reptile or amphibian show and you will get a sense of just how many morphs can be created from seemingly uniform, humble animals. In nature, many species have populations that vary slightly in coloration or other traits due to the local habitat, but to see animals of the same species with completely different coloration is rare.

## A NOTE ABOUT NAMES

In this book we don't capitalize common names, except when a place or person is commemorated. Other handbooks do, however, and our sidewinder will be their Sidewinder. In scientific names, the genus is capitalized but the species epithet is not, and no matter what the common name, a sidewinder is *Crotalus cerastes*.

## MORPHS, SUBSPECIES, AND SPECIES IN ACTION

At White Sands National Park in New Mexico, three species of lizards have evolved blanched coloration to blend in with the gypsum dune habitat. Other lizards of the same species that don't live in the dunes are not white. How should we consider these white lizards: morphs, subspecies, or a separate species altogether? The answer, like many things in biology, is that it depends. After intense study, biologists have determined that the three lizards in the dunes are at different stages of the speciation process. The southwestern fence lizard (*Sceloporus cowlesi*) is simply considered a different color morph compared to the surrounding species. A certain earless lizard (*Holbrookia maculata ruthveni*) is distinct enough that it is considered a subspecies of the lesser earless lizard. And the little white whiptail (*Aspidoscelis gypsi*) is so far diverged from non-dunes whiptails that it has been elevated to species status.

Hikers in White Sands National Park might see the local subspecies of earless lizard, specially adapted to blend in with the pale environment.

## How big is "big"?

Because tails can break off, naturalists often measure herps by snout-to-vent length (SVL). That basically means the length of the head and body, down to the cloaca, the reproductive organ near the start of the tail. This book gives measurements in various ways, making clear whether the size includes the tail or not. We always use inches or feet in this book (since that is what most people are familiar with), but in-house, we three authors are more likely to converse in metric. If you're a young reader hoping to enter into the sciences, we encourage you to become bilingual in your measurement systems.

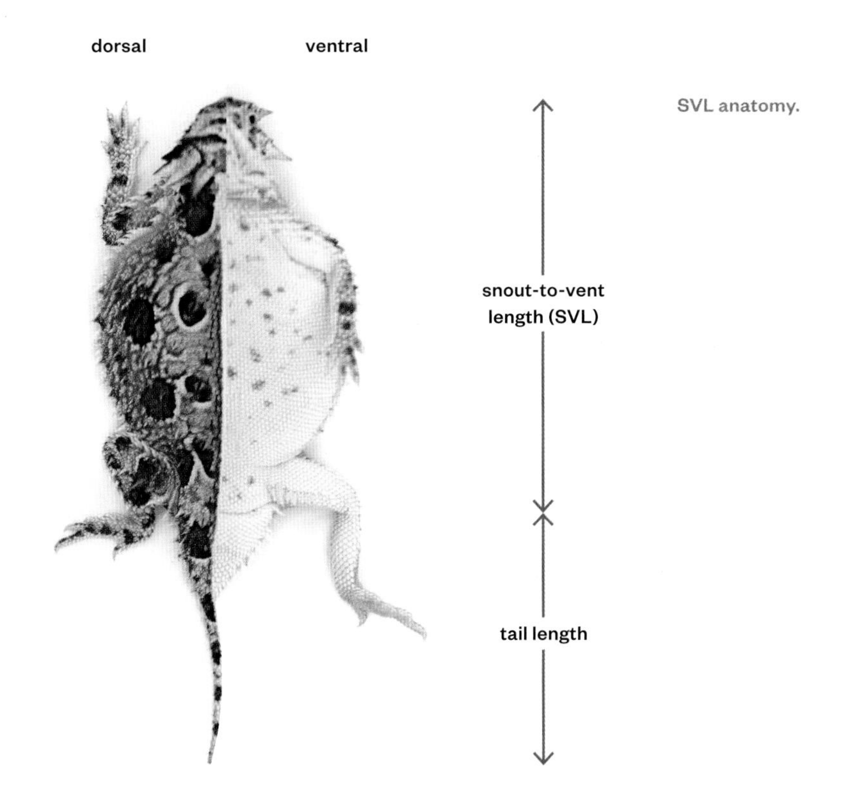


SVL anatomy.

# Sexual diversity, sex determination, and mating systems

When we think about sexual diversity in reptiles and amphibians, perhaps the first thing to clarify is the meaning of biological sex—the genetic, hormonal, and organismal characters that define an individual's sex.

In human culture, we have a separate concept known as gender identity, which can (but may not always) align with one's biological sex. And of course, the concepts of sex and gender are distinct from human sexual attraction: all three of these concepts are best viewed as spectra in our species. It's important not to impose our biases about sex, gender, and sexual attraction onto other systems, but to appreciate all the diversity found in our own species and others. When we talk about reptiles and amphibians, we will refer to their biological sex only; as far as we know, reptiles and amphibians don't have socially informed gender roles, but we are learning more about these topics every day.

## Sexual diversity

Most species of amphibians and reptiles have two sexes, which we typically refer to as male and female. By males we usually mean the sex that invests more lower-cost gametes (i.e., sperm), whereas females invest fewer, higher-cost gametes (eggs). Some species of whiptails in the Southwest are comprised only of females, and they reproduce through parthenogenesis, a system in which females make clones of themselves instead of mating with males. Parthenogenesis occurs across the animal kingdom, in species as distantly related as termites and fish.

In addition to single-sex species, the latest research suggests that sex reversals, in which a male animal shifts

into a female or vice versa, are quite common. Some of the chemicals we use on our lawns lead to sex reversals in frogs, but such a switch in frogs can occur without chemicals present, too—it might be a completely natural evolutionary process.

This whiptail lizard is a female-only species that reproduces through parthenogenesis.

## Sex determination

In reptiles, sex can be determined in two ways: by genetics or by temperature. The genetic pathway is familiar to us: most people recognize that human sexual diversity (again, *not* gender diversity) is in part determined by our genetics—specifically, the type of chromosomes we have. In humans, we have X chromosomes and Y chromosomes, which in different combinations produce different sexes. In reptiles, some lizards and turtles and pythons also have X and Y chromosomes, which determine their sex. Other lizards (like bearded dragons) and snakes have different types of chromosomes, Z and W, and their combinations dictate which are born female and which male.

Another pathway that dictates whether embryos develop as male or female is the temperature at which they incubate. This route—temperature-dependent sex determination—happens in reptiles, many invertebrates, and some fish. In many turtles, males develop at low temperatures and females at high temps. The opposite is true in the tuatara, a New Zealand endemic that also happens to be the closest ancestor to all other lizards. In alligators, males develop at intermediate temps and females at low and high temps.

Recent research has shown that these two pathways can work together; in Australian skinks, some embryos may have XX chromosomes (genetically female), but when incubated at low temps, they develop functional male reproductive organs. Other environmental factors, like pH, habitat color, and number of other developing embryos can affect sexual development and sex ratios.

## Mating systems

Reptiles and amphibians exhibit diversity in mating systems as well. In many frog species, males expend energy calling, while females assess individuals based on the quality of the call to make mating decisions. Male and female lizards use showy colors and displays such as pushups to defend territory and attract mates. Some turtles use their claws to signal they are interested in mating. Female snakes release pheromones that let males know they are ready to mate. In some species like rattlesnakes, males may engage in combat over mates. In other species like anacondas, females will sometimes eat males after they have mated. In many herp species, assuming one does not devour the other, both males and females will undergo multiple matings per season.

Once individuals have decided on a mate, how do they actually go about the process? Herps have a single organ, the cloaca, through which they mate and excrete waste. In frogs, the mating posture, or amplexus, goes like this: the male frog holds onto the female from behind, in order to get into position to fertilize the female's eggs as they emerge from her cloaca. The eggs will incubate outside,

Sea turtles live in the ocean but nest on land, like these olive ridley sea turtles coming ashore in Nicaragua.

and depending on the species, the male or female will care for them as they develop into tadpoles, then froglets, and ultimately frogs. Turtles use amplexus too, and in sea turtles, females decide when their eggs have been sufficiently fertilized.

Male lizards and snakes have hemipenes, a pair (usually) of sexual organs that are kept within the cloaca except for mating. The male will insert one of the hemipenes into the female's cloaca during mating to fertilize her eggs. Females then hold onto the eggs as they develop, and many species then lay the fertilized eggs through the cloaca and allow them to hatch. But in some species females retain the eggs until they hatch inside of her; this is a modified version of live birth that tends to occur in cooler environments.

Many reptiles and amphibians also engage in non-sexual mating actions. In the aforementioned all-female whiptails, two females will mate to induce reproduction, even though no fertilization occurs. Garter snakes often form mating balls, where large numbers of snakes, usually males, will gather and attempt to mate. Many males try to mate with other males during this process. Male toads don't discriminate during the mating season—they are often observed attempting to mate with other males of their species and even different species altogether.

## Infectious diseases and conservation

Most scientists agree: our species is affecting the planet at an unprecedented rate. Reptiles and amphibians are feeling the effects of climate change too, from loss of habitat to the emergence of novel pathogens.

Among the biggest threats to our native amphibians and reptiles are diseases caused by fungi. Globalization, including trade and travel, has exacerbated these diseases and caused them to spread far. That includes chytrid fungus (aka Bd, short for its scientific name), which has led to massive die-offs in frogs and resulted in total extinction of some species. Another fungus in the chytrid family, Bsal, is impacting salamanders. The effects are similar to chytrid in frogs: fungal spores in the skin affect the animal's ability to perform key physiological processes and can result in death. A third fungus causes snake fungal disease. This fungus creates lesions that can penetrate through the hard, outer scales of snake's skin. Some snakes are able to fight off the fungus when they shed, but not all are so lucky. This disease was discovered in timber

A probable victim of pesticides, this frog has a small fifth limb.

rattlesnakes on the east coast of North America in 2006 and has been moving steadily westward since.

Contaminated water creates other problems. One example is atrazine, a chemical found in herbicides and one of the most common pollutants in drinking water. Recent research showed that atrazine disrupted normal hormone pathways: the testosterone levels of male leopard frogs became so low that their reproductive organs shrank, and they were unable to produce sperm. This results in skewed sex ratios: instead of the usual balance of males to females, there are far fewer reproductively active males, which affects the number of offspring that can be produced.

Humans have a stake here: things that harm smaller animals may have unintended consequences for us, too.

Other threats to reptiles and amphibians include habitat loss and degradation, and fragmentation due to development. Cattle grazing and trampling affects grassland

### WHAT CAN YOU DO TO HELP?

One of the best things you can do to help your local herps is to be a keen observer. If you see an animal that looks or acts strange, take notes, or better yet, photos: scientists can use these to track the spread of diseases or document new threats. You can upload these photos to free apps such as iNaturalist or HerpMapper, where researchers can easily see your observations. And when it comes to herps, it's better to look and not touch—your hands touch a lot of things throughout the day, and there is a chance you could accidentally infect an animal with something that you didn't even know was there. If you are permitted to handle animals, always leave them where you found them. When recreating, stay on trails so you don't accidentally degrade habitat for herps. Drive slowly and carefully on roads where herps are abundant: you never know what could be underfoot (or under-tire). And if you see a rattlesnake or other animal near your home, never try to kill it: use a hose to encourage it to move away or call a professional relocation service.

specialists and riparian species. Many herps are hit by cars when they attempt road crossings. And some species, such as rattlesnakes or Gila monsters, are persecuted simply for existing.

## Natives vs. non-natives

Biologically, the North American continent is a mix of native species and introduced ones. In some cases, like with red foxes and red-legged frogs, California might have the same species but from different points of origins, creating native and non-native populations. For herps, non-native species can affect native ones, and that includes red-eared sliders (page 98), American bullfrogs (page 82), and African clawed frogs (page 63).

Red-eared sliders are fine as pets but become a plague if released into the wild.

Mediterranean geckos are now established in parts of Southern California, but their impact has yet to be seen.

Non-natives—and in some cases, invasive species—can really be harmful. Some species arrive in shipping containers or the root balls of garden plants, and since some geckos practice parthenogenesis, a new population establishes itself easily.

In the case of red-eared sliders, the founding population came from released pets. Please, please, please, never release pets or any other animal into a place it doesn't belong. Even if it does not eat up all the lesser-sized critters, it could spread a disease. (This is a particular concern for desert tortoises.) By not releasing pets back into nature, you will not only prevent them from facing a hungry and miserable death, but you could also save the lives of thousands of other animals whose native habitat happens to be your release site. In the name of them all: thank you!

## Getting started

Birding is easier with good binoculars, but to see your first herps you just need curiosity, time in the field, and a willingness to pay attention. You can spot lizards in Reno or downtown Los Angeles; Seattle is a good base if you're looking for the Puget Sound garter snake, a blue form of the common garter snake.

A mobile phone or camera is good for documenting new finds. We always recommend a pocket notebook, but that's as much to capture poetry and general ideas as it is to log who/what/where/when details. If you're out after dark—fun and highly recommended—back up your headlamp with a handheld light; we're fans of the always-have-a-spare-light philosophy. You'll need boots if the trail is rough or wellies if it's especially mucky. Otherwise, any hiking shoes will do. And we always say to bring twice as much water as you could possibly need when traveling in the desert.

Depending on location and time of year, we usually have a pole in the car to nudge snakes off paved roads so the next car that comes along doesn't squish them. (Be especially careful to use a long pole if trying to relocate a rattlesnake—better yet, leave it alone if you don't have experience.) Binoculars help get closer looks at turtles and lizards. Many frogs and toads can just be caught by hand if you're reasonably quick,

To get started, you just need some hiking shoes (purple nail polish optional).

but be careful—some toads have toxins that can hurt you, and similarly, many of the things we humans carry on our hands can harm amphibians.

Really, you don't need much more than this book and a desire to go out and see what treasures the day (or night) has to offer. As you flip through the pages, we hope you're as excited to meet new species in the field as we are to share them with you.

## Where to go herping

Backyards and city parks are great places to start. If it has a stream, better yet. Major national parks like Olympic, Death Valley, or the Grand Canyon provide lists of reptiles and amphibians, and often give habitat notes to help you refine your search. Other parks like Craters of the Moon National Monument and Preserve in Idaho or Columbia National Wildlife Refuge in eastern Washington will be just as good or better for herps, but you may need to combine park lists with websites like iNaturalist to get a good study plan before setting off.

Seasons matter, as does the location. You can find newts and other salamanders in Portland in January, but in the desert, lizards and snakes will be easier to find in spring and summer. Where you go depends on how much time you have, how far you are willing to drive, and what you most want to see first. Rather than location, let's think more about time of day.

[above]
Grand Canyon National Park is home to eight amphibian and 41 reptile species.

[left] As the day warms up, these garden walls will be perfect for watching lizards.

## Herping during the day

Herping will change the way you look the world. Piles of rocks and scraps of plywood on the side of the road will never be the same because you will stare at them thinking about the species that live there. Reptiles in particular are well adapted to diurnal life. They will be more heat tolerant than the species you find at night, though also faster and more skittish. However, you will have the advantage of having a pair of daylight-adapted, stereoscopic eyes and maybe even 10-power binoculars.

In most areas, daylight will give you a bonanza of lizard species. Spiny lizards and horned lizards will likely occur anywhere you are in the western United States. If you are in the Southwest, you can go for some gourmet, highly specialized species like the fringe-toed lizards that occur only in the Mojave National Preserve and other sand dune areas; chuckwallas, desert iguanas, earless lizards, zebra-tailed lizards, and leopard lizards are also active here.

Success! When you're done, be sure to put the log back the way you found it, carefully, without squishing your new friend.

Some of the most beautiful snakes are active during the day. Patch-nosed snakes, racers, whipsnakes, and the coachwhip are diurnal. They use their fast movements to catch fast-moving prey, which includes many lizards and other snakes. Despite being mostly nocturnal or crepuscular (dawn and dusk), rattlesnakes are always a possibility. During cooler months, rattlesnakes will be active during the day. They can also be found resting in the shade just outside burrows at the base of bushes.

As you gain experience, you will find more and more herps. As you start, the inability of reptiles to regulate their body temperature on their own is a fact you will exploit to your advantage. Many species need to bask first thing in the morning. Rocky outcrops are great places to look. Move toward the rocks slowly and scan the top for pointy silhouettes, but do practice stealthy field craft: some lizards will quickly disappear if you are moving too fast or making too much noise. Side-blotched lizards are relatively abundant wherever they occur and will usually be sitting on the top of warm rocks in the morning. The best way to spook a basking lizard is to let your shadow fall over it, so try to avoid this.

Don't forget to bring a flashlight or a small mirror. Inspect crevices in the rock walls, burrows, and dark corners of vegetation clumps. In narrow canyons, look for areas with shade and water accumulation. Frogs and other amphibians will spend the day in these areas to avoid dehydration.

In open areas, medium-sized isolated rocks are preferred by species like collared lizards. Make use of binoculars to search several dozens of yards ahead of you since these species flee easily. For our largest lizard, the chuckwalla, larger rock outcrops and old lava fields with crevices big enough for their stocky bodies will be preferred.

One of herpers' most recognizable behaviors is "flipping," which basically consists of turning over anything you can, albeit carefully. Can we say it again? *Carefully*. During the hottest part of the day, many species will look for protection under rocks, old signs, plywood, and dead vegetation. Many nocturnal species will also spend the day in these places, so you also have a chance to find a sleepy night lizard or a banded gecko. Always assume that someone is living under what you pick up and proceed cautiously: be careful not to harm them (and to be sure they don't harm you). Many species require very specific microclimates for spending the day, so whether it is rocks or trash, always return the objects to the exact same place you found them, after placing the animal gently underneath once again.

A young herper celebrates the end of a productive field day.

Last, we note that daytime is also good for scouting new areas that you can visit at night.

## Herping at night

Remember that you were flipping logs and old metal during the day? Well, good news! You probably won't have to do that when you look for herps at night. In deserts and low-elevation areas, many reptiles will take advantage of more tolerable night temperatures to go out to hunt and patrol their territories for mates. Most amphibians will

The Milky Way rises above an Arizona stream; headlamps reveal after-dark herpers.

also crawl out of their shaded resting areas and increase their activity, taking advantage of both the lower temperatures and the lack of strong sunlight, which dehydrates their sensitive skin.

Herps also adopt nocturnal strategies that keep them relatively safe from birds and other predators, but some species are better adapted to nighttime than others. The well-named night snake and most rattlesnakes have adaptations to nighttime that involve larger pupils to catch as much light as possible and, in the case of rattlesnakes, thermal sensors near the nose to detect prey in full darkness. Other semi-fossorial species like groundsnakes, coral snakes, and threadsnakes all venture out at night. And amphibians will most likely attempt to commute from their burrows to ponds at night.

When it comes to seeing things at night, your goals will vary by time of year. In spring, look for medium to small bodies of water, which will be prime herping spots. Usually the sound of dozens of toads and frogs will guide you to them. Slow-flowing parts of streams are also good places to look. Creeks and riverbeds are like highways for many herps. Wherever you find frogs, there is a good chance that predator reptiles will be there too. Most garter snakes will hunt day and night depending on temperature and will be happy to capture almost any amphibian you can imagine.

As a herper, few things are better than the opportunity of road cruising at night on low-traffic roads in the desert or the foothills. Many reptiles will feel attracted to the warm pavement on cooler nights. Road cruising also maximizes the amount of area you can cover at night. Look for coiled rattlesnakes right on the edge of the road. Always be careful of traffic and keep speed down so you can brake safely at the first sighting. Remember that other people might not be expecting stopped vehicles, so make sure to pull over, turn on your flashers, use a headlamp, and keep everyone safe.

Other smaller species will be very difficult to spot from a moving car. In parks and campgrounds, paved trails will allow you to spot small animals better. Rocky areas are great places to look for herps with smaller home ranges like banded geckos and night lizards.

And when you see something good, if you're lucky enough to get a picture, do please share your sighting. But for now, keep reading! This introduction concludes with more information on community science options.

Being out at night means encountering other fun animals, like this cute kangaroo rat.

## Common sense about rattlesnakes

Just to be super clear about one thing, a rattlesnake—even a small one—can kill you. **Do not mess around with rattlesnakes.** Luckily, most bites are preventable, and, if you are bitten, with prompt treatment, almost all bites are survivable.

Take any posted warnings very seriously.

Let's start with what (and where) the risks are. The western side of the continent does not have any cottonmouths or copperheads, and our one coral snake (page 196) generally stays out of sight and is non-aggressive—nationwide, less than one fatal bite per every 40 years can be linked to coral snakes.

That does, however, leave rattlesnakes (pages 182–195). Rattlesnakes are fascinating creatures, and they don't want to bite you and waste their precious time and venom when they could have a tastier meal, like a kangaroo rat or small rabbit. Stories of people being "chased down by rattlers" are simply not true—almost all rattlesnake bites are avoidable if you respect the animal and give it space. If you see one on the road, don't try to move it; and even if you think it has been killed, it can still bite out of reflex (and may not be dead), so don't try to cut off the rattles or hold it up for a trophy shot. If you see a rattlesnake while hiking, don't pick it up. Don't move it off the trail. Don't lean close to get a better picture. *Give them space.*

Gender and risky behavior come into play here: the statistics show a distinct (and self-selected) pattern of victims. Nationally, of 9,000 emergency room snake bite visits per year, men account for 70% of the patients, and, of those, most are aged 21 to 39. Those few who die (typically only a few people per year) tend to be older, due to complicating, non-bite factors, but based on total ER visits, it seems that most snake bites happen to young men. This implies that behavior patterns must be a root cause of most snake bites. **Do not mess around with rattlesnakes**—guys, we are talking to *you*.

Using a telephoto lens, co-author Erin Westeen keeps a safe distance from this western diamondback.

Yes, you can still be bitten while hiking, but nationally, many cases are preventable. Common sense matters, in this and all things. When hiking, pay attention: don't step where you can't see. If scrambling, watch where you're putting your hands. If you're going to rest on a log, look first before sitting down (or squatting, if going to the loo out of doors).

Thousands and thousands of people hike many tens of thousands of miles per year without incident. Yet, of course, incidents do happen. If you're bitten by a snake, do these things:

- Stop hiking and move away from the snake. (Don't run and risk tripping. Go slow.)

- Assume you have been envenomated; don't wait for symptoms to develop.

- Immediately phone for help. No service? Send somebody to call for you if it is close.

- While waiting, be still. Keep the wound lower than the heart.

- Do **not** cut open the bite site and try to suck out poison or increase bleeding to "flush the poison." The senior author remembers when a snake bite kit included a scalpel and suction cups. You can slice a tendon—or worse. **Do not cut anything.**

- Do **not** apply a tourniquet.

- Do **not** try to catch or kill the snake in question.

- If the bite is on a hand, take off watch and rings: extreme swelling may be coming soon.

- If you have a Sharpie or pen, mark bite site and time of bite on your skin.

- If you have a notebook, write down details about the snake, to help ID it in the hospital.

▶ If you're alone with no phone service, time to walk back *slowly*. Drink some water, take your keys and phone, dump whatever you don't immediately need, and hike out slowly.

The good news is that most bite victims survive.

In case you're wondering about absolute risk, in the United States, about five people a year die from snake bites. To put that in context, lightning strikes kill 25 to 50 people a year, 10,000 people are killed each year by drunk drivers, 100,000 people a year are killed or wounded by guns, and dogs bite 4.7 million people a year, of whom 800,000 need medical attention.

Don't let a fear of snakes keep you from hiking. Hiking is one of the best things you can do for your heart, your mind, and your soul.

## Community science options

Ever wonder what species you could find if you take the next exit to that lonely road beside the interstate? Or how range maps are drawn in field guides? Not too long ago, most data were based on museum specimens collected by naturalists during expeditions. Since these expeditions could cover only a limited area in a limited amount of time, many species' actual distributions were underestimated.

Nowadays, the devices in the palms of our hands allow us to share our observations, keep track of our sightings, and help science by reporting what we've seen. Community science not only allows you to collectively improve the range maps of species but also helps provide a better understanding of life cycles, poorly observed behaviors (including interactions with other species), and the spread of disease.

Several platforms allow enthusiast naturalists to provide useful data to scientists and other users. Some resemble social media apps; others are more specialized in terms of audience or the type of data that can be submitted. You can install them on your phone and use the camera and GPS on it to record the specific locality of your sightings.

Hear a treefrog? Smart phones let you document the find with video and audio.

One of the most recognizable platforms is iNaturalist.org. It is a preferred source to check for species reports when planning a trip in search of that species of lizard you haven't seen or photographed. iNaturalist will also compile the sightings by time, so you can look for your target during the best season. Focused on amphibians and reptiles, HerpMapper.org is another important tool. Both HerpMapper and iNaturalist can suggest identification from photos. HerpMapper may be the best choice for rare or endangered species because exact locations are not publicly available.

Species accounts in books are limited by the number of photos and pages, showing only one or a few photos of each species. With millions of records are uploaded every day, community science platforms are also great sources to find photographs for identification. Species like the rosy boa have expansive ranges and numerous color morphs and subspecies, so looking at other records near yours will provide much more useful photos to ID your own sightings.

Here is how to make the most out of your records. When posting a record of an observation, make sure to include as many details as you can. Besides the GPS location and time (which are usually recorded by your phone), be sure to include notes about the overall habitat, microhabitat, behavior, and any interaction with other species. Photos should include features that can be used for identification. In a perfect world, you will be able to photograph animals from multiple angles and show details like toes in amphibians and head scales in snakes. In an imperfect world—the one the authors live in most of the time—just do the best you can. Miss a detail? There is always next time.

To get help on an iNaturalist ID, mark it as the closest group you know for sure (e.g., snakes, turtles), and the members of the platform will give you a hand. Many researchers are active members on these platforms, which makes them great places to get in contact with professionals and let them know about your sightings, offer to volunteer for field work, or just ask them about some interesting behavior you observed. Good science needs good data, and the more context for your sighting you include, the more useful it will be.

Keep in mind that when looking for herps, you will encounter many other non-herp species. iNaturalist will accept reports of any living organism on the planet, but if you have seen some interesting kangaroo rats or tree voles, mammalwatching.com archives mammal reports. If you're herping and birding on the same trip, eBird will gladly accept your bird notes.

In all cases, please join the conversation: share your experiences and smile broadly when you realize you have documented something noteworthy. As the pages of this book will say over and over, when it comes to reptiles and amphibians, there is a lot we have yet to figure out.

# AMPHIBIANS

# Pacific giant salamanders

*Dicamptodon* spp.

FUN FACT

They can chirp, growl, or even give a small bark.

| SIZE | FOOD | SPECIES IN OUR AREA |
|---|---|---|
| 2–7 inches; with tail, up to 12 inches | slugs, worms, insects, eggs, rodents, other salamanders | 4: Idaho giant salamander (*D. aterrimus*), Cope's giant salamander (*D. copei*), California giant salamander (*D. ensatus*), coastal giant salamander (*D. tenebrosus*) |

You can tell Pacific giant salamanders by their size—with tail, up to 12 inches long. This is a California giant salamander.

For a salamander, this is a robust-bodied, stout-limbed, broad-nosed "lizard-like" animal. The genus members are collectively known as Pacific giant salamanders, but the four species are distinct from each other genetically, even if all four tend to be orangey brown with a marbling of dark blotches (or dark with tan blotches, in the case of Idaho giant salamander).

Giant salamanders are nocturnal sit-and-wait predators—if they can fit it in their mouth, they will try to eat it. Range follows the coastal fog belt. From south to north, the southernmost species, the California giant salamander, centers on the Bay Area, from Santa Cruz to Sonoma. The coastal giant salamander starts north of that, and its range extends through California to Oregon and Washington and the bottom edge of British Columbia. Cope's giant salamander crosses that range at right angles, going west to east from the Olympic Peninsula into the Cascades.

Heading east there is a rain shadow gap in eastern Washington, then a fourth species, the Idaho giant salamander, can be found in northern Idaho. It is now mostly confined to headwater streams, because in lower, more accessible forests, aggressive logging muddies the rivers, raises the temperature, and unbalances the ecosystem so badly that they can no longer survive. Clear water and wet forests—that is the primary habitat for all these species.

What wants to eat them? Predators, says one source, include fish, garter snakes, weasels, and water shrews. (Death by water shrew seems an especially obscure way to meet one's fate.) To defend themselves, all four can squawk or growl, lash their tails, and bite vigorously. In addition, all four have toxic skin secretions.

## NOT A HELLBENDER

This group comprises the largest terrestrial salamanders in North America. From New York down to Alabama, there is also the famous hellbender salamander (aka snot otter), 20 inches or more, but it is primarily aquatic.

Pacific giant salamanders share similar life cycles. Adults typically stay within a few hundred feet of streams, venturing out on the forest floor only on rainy nights and during wet winter days. Adults are also found under rocks in streams and under moisture-protecting cover inside the forest, such as under rocks, logs, dense leaf litter, and even pieces of plywood.

The Pacific Northwest is full of salamander habitat (and salamander species).

They mate and breed in spring. Males deposit sperm packets (spermatophores) underwater, and females use those to fertilize up to 200 eggs that they lay inside an underwater nest chamber. To keep anything from eating up her investment, the female guards the eggs until they hatch. Larvae are born in the water, where they swim using an enlarged tail and breathe using gills. The aquatic

Up close and personal with a California giant salamander.

larvae transform into four-legged salamanders that live on the ground and breathe air with lungs. One exception are the neotenic adults (paedomorphs); they retain their gills and continue to live in water. In some streams, gilled adults may outnumber the transformed, welcome-to-land individuals.

### WHAT'S IN A NAME?

The Olympic Peninsula species, Cope's giant salamander, is named for American naturalist Edward Drinker Cope (1840–1897). For every organism, there is supposed to be a museum specimen that is the voucher or reference unit, what is known as the holotype. *The Eponym Dictionary of Reptiles* (2011) provides this interesting detail. "In his will [Cope] asked that his body should be used as the holotype of *Homo sapiens*, but his skeleton was found to be unsuitable because of disease; it was rumored that he died of syphilis, but the cause is more likely to have been prostatitis complicated by self-medication using formalin and belladonna." That is, he tried to extend his life by drinking formaldehyde mixed with a toxic and hallucinogenic form of nightshade.

Kids, definitely do not try that at home.

# newts

*Taricha* spp.

FUN FACT

A juvenile newt is called an eft.

| SIZE | FOOD | SPECIES IN OUR AREA |
|---|---|---|
| 4–7 inches including tail | insects, worms, eggs, small fish | 4: rough-skinned newt (*T. granulosa*), red-bellied newt (*T. rivularis*), Sierra newt (*T. sierrae*), California newt (*T. torosa*) |

**PEASANT [pointing at an accused witch]:**
**She turned me into a newt!**
**KING ARTHUR [skeptical]: A newt?**
**PEASANT: Well, I got better.**

—*Monty Python and the Holy Grail*

What is a newt, exactly? Often mistaken for lizards, these amphibians are actually salamanders and haven't been closely related to lizards for 350 million years. They are often nocturnal, and the four species in our area all look similar: brown back, orange belly, and large, Gollum-round eyes. With stocky bodies, wide toes, and a lumbering gait, newts are quite cute. But be careful, as they are toxic! Males can grow "nuptial pads" on their fleshy toes in the breeding season to help them grip their partners.

**Newts have a rubbery, gummy-bear body plan.**

Moist or rainy nights are best for newt-hunting; this California newt was found near Berkeley.

## HIGHWAY 1, NOT ROUTE 66 (AND WHY TO SLOW DOWN)

The most widespread species of this group, the rough-skinned newt, ranges up and down the Pacific Coast from Alaska to Santa Cruz, and all four species stay west of the Cascades and the Sierra Crest. Seattle and Portland and Berkeley and the Merced River going into Yosemite all have rough-skinned newts, but there are no naturally occurring newts in Arizona, Utah, Nevada, or Colorado.

Of the others, red-bellied newts occur only in Northern California, both north of San Francisco and also around Santa Cruz. The Sierra newt does indeed live in the Sierra Nevada foothills and forests; it tolerates drier living conditions than do the others. The California newt is coastal and southern: a subspecies lives in the Southern Sierra, but the rest prefer the coast from Mendocino south to San Diego. It is the species one looks for around Los Angeles.

The one exception to the coast-only rule is a cluster of rough-skinned newt records centered on Moscow, Idaho. The idea of newts in the Palouse seems a bit like an oxymoron. Do they feel lonely or brave, being so far east of the others?

To see a newt in the wild, just think wet. Since newts are salamanders, that means newts will generally be in and around streams, under damp rocks, and waiting for rainy nights more than they will be hoping for Santa Ana winds and noon light. To find a good spot near you, look up *Taricha* on iNaturalist or search the advice shared in the Field Herp Forum. Even better: find a new spot nobody knows about, just by exploring little-used paths along shady streams. You can find newts even inside the Portland city limits.

Threats to newts include habitat loss, water pollution (they have very sensitive skin), and exotic fish introduced to their streams. One less obvious threat is speeding cars. Thousands of newts die on roads each year as they leave their home territory in search of mates. One recent iNaturalist report from Los Gatos (near San Jose) shares this sad reality: "I found 230 dead newts on Alma Bridge Road this morning in 2 hours." That tells us it's time to slow down and look at the scenery—both the wildlife and our inner sense of peace will appreciate it.

Wet forests are perfect for newts and other salamanders.

## PLEASE DON'T LICK THE NEWTS

In each of the species, the newt's color pattern serves two purposes. Dark-on-top is basic camouflage, and the orange bellies can be displayed in times of stress to warn off hungry snakes and eager children. The warning is needed because newts produce tetrodotoxin, a neurotoxin that shuts down the heart and lungs of potential newt-snacking predators. How they make this toxin is not yet fully understood; they might sequester it from microbes. In any case, if you handle any of our newts (which we don't encourage), make sure you don't have any open cuts and do wash your hands afterward—this toxin works on humans, too.

Their nemesis is the garter snake (page 229). As newts evolved defenses, garter snakes countered that by evolving immunity to tetrodotoxins.

This fact reminds us that evolution is always a high-ante poker game. "I see your bucket of poison and raise you three spines and a detachable tail. *Call.*"

# slender salamanders

*Batrachoseps* spp.

**FUN FACT**
Young have gills while inside the egg but hatch as air-breathers.

| SIZE | FOOD | SPECIES IN OUR AREA |
|---|---|---|
| 1–2.5 inches, plus a tail often longer than body | snails, small insects (mites, springtails, beetles), spiders | 22, almost all with restricted ranges |

This is one of the book's two lungless salamander species clusters, and like the ensatina complex (see next entry), slender salamanders breathe through their skin and the linings of their mouth. Not having to fill up your chest with lungs makes it easier to feed, breed, and rest in slim, damp places, like between tree bark and a rotting log or in the crevices of mossy cliffs. Slender salamanders are able to exploit microhabitats, finding moisture even inside the rotting base of an old yucca, or on a north-facing hillside where late snowmelt keeps the leaf litter damp.

Slender salamanders are so thin and wiggly, they look like worms.

### NON-DARWINIAN DARWINIAN EVOLUTION

Evolutionary biologists note that this array of 20-plus species does not represent an adaptive radiation, in which, for example, one finch on a lava-coated island evolves into two species, one of which is good at cracking open small seeds, and the other, with a different beak, is better at finding and eating large seeds. Instead, this array represents *non*-adaptive radiation: the plurality of slender salamanders speciated not because of any major habitat differences between one site and the next but because of geographic separation. There simply was not enough gene flow from isolated group to isolated group, so now we have an abundance of ecologically similar salamanders, each of which represents a different twig on the tree of life.

That means that there is a San Simeon slender salamander, a different one in the Inyo Mountains, another one in the Santa Lucia Mountains, and yet another on the Kern Plateau. The Oregon slender salamander prefers closed-canopy red cedar, Douglas-fir, and maple forests, though it can make do in post-logging successional forests and even suburban parks. It is only found in north-central Oregon, on both sides of the Cascades.

**This group breathes through their skin, hence their alternative common name, the lungless salamanders.**

Sometimes checking the scientific names reveals interesting history. Tehachapi slender salamander (*Batrachoseps stebbinsi*) has a specific epithet that remembers a famous herpetology professor. The Hell Hollow slender salamander (*B. diabolicus*) has an epithet that sounds ominous indeed, but it is merely a nod to the

From wrens to shrews, forests like this one hold salamanders—and many other treasures besides.

type location in Maricopa County, California. And of course behavior can inspire names, such as the gregarious slender salamander (*B. gregarius*); in this species, females share communal nests.

## HOW WE KNOW WHAT LIVES WHERE

The short answer to "How do we know what lives where?" is "Well, we don't, not yet, not completely." If you want to contribute to science right away, head out and look for things—but do your "looking" in places nobody else has visited yet. A forum for herpers was sharing all the places that the Tehachapi slender salamander was being found, places it should "not" have been, if we just went by previous reports. As one of the posts pointed out, "It is important to avoid having assumptions about habitat use become confirmed dogma because nobody bothered to look anywhere else."

Academic study can help direct energies and give context for discoveries, but we hope amateurs reading this book are encouraged as well. There is a place for everybody in this conversation, and if you don't have a Ph.D., don't feel bad—Charles Darwin didn't either.

# ensatina salamander

*Ensatina eschscholtzii*

FUN FACT

One of the best examples worldwide of a ring species complex.

| SIZE | FOOD | SPECIES IN OUR AREA |
| --- | --- | --- |
| 1.5–3 inches, plus a tail of 1–2 inches | spiders, beetles, crickets, worms, snails | 1 |

Ensatinas are lungless salamanders (they breathe through their skin and the linings of their mouths), and because they have no lungs, they can be long, flexible, and thin—almost as thin as a tiny snake. In fact, getting rid of your lungs means you can be thin enough to exploit the moist-crevice niche of habitat choices. Another group in this book, the slender salamanders (page 54), has evolved the same way.

Colors vary. Many ensatinas are pink, orange, or reddish, but some subspecies can be all black with yellow blotches or slate gray with orange. Some of those forms may be distinct species—or else, maybe not. Authorities have yet to come to consensus.

**LIKE ANTEATERS, SALAMANDERS GO "ZOT"**

In the comic strip *B.C.*, the anteater character goes "Zot!" when his tongue spears a juicy ant. (Zot is also the "war cry" of UC Irvine, whose mascot is an anteater.) Ensatinas might say this too, at least in the quiet of their own minds, since their tongues are covered with a sticky mucus and can dart forward with agile dexterity

to zap out-of-reach prey. The last thought of some small, unlucky beetle might be, "Wait a minute, you can't do that. You're not a frog!"

This is one of the more widely distributed groups in the book. The range starts in western British Columbia and generally stays west of the Cascades in Washington and Oregon. In California it splits into two strands: the left side follows the coast ranges into Baja, and the right follows both sides of the Sierra Nevada down to Tehachapi. This distribution in California, in which the salamanders encircle the Central Valley but do not enter it, is typical of a ring-species complex: each subspecies can mate with the adjacent one, but the subspecies that meet at the base of the "ring" are no longer able to interbreed.

**Ensatinas form a ring species complex: each population can interbreed with the one closest to it, but at each end, the populations no longer share direct gene flow.**

Damp places, hidden places are preferred: and so, under logs, under boards, under stones, burrowed down under thick leaf litter—that is where ensatinas thrive, and that includes understories of redwood forest, oak woodland, and even regular chaparral.

Truly waterlogged soil is too saturated, so this species wants the Goldilocks just-rightness of protected and damp, but not soggy and definitely not desiccated. In productive habitat, ensatinas may live 15 years and, in all that time, never leave a 100-foot circle.

## SLIMEBAG DEFENSE STRATEGIES

To find salamanders, go out on mild, rainy nights, but it's better for them if you don't handle them much or even at all. One defensive strategy is they can secrete a sticky mucous, and it's such a thick coating of slime, it can muck up the mouthparts of small snakes. You don't want it on your hands, either, and if the ensatinas get dried out from being handled (or if they get too badly stressed), it is definitely not good for their health. Wetting your hands before a brief moment of show and tell with the kids is probably fine, but for this and all the species in the book, be aware of what the animal itself is experiencing. Hippocrates had it right: "First, do not harm."

Look for these salamanders under logs or near streams. They range from Canada to Baja.

# tailed frogs

## *Ascaphus* spp.

**FUN FACT**

Tadpoles take two to four years to mature into adult frogs.

| SIZE | FOOD | SPECIES IN OUR AREA |
|---|---|---|
| 1–2 inches | tadpoles graze algae; adults eat insects, spiders, snails | 2: Rocky Mountain tailed frog (*A. montanus*), coastal tailed frog (*A. truei*) |

"Frog-spotting, like bird-watching, takes patience and perseverance"—so says an article in *National Geographic*. Here is a frog that tests both patience *and* perseverance. The tailed frog is small, silent, nocturnal, and found only in swift, steep, cold rivers. In comparison to those challenges, looking for spotted owls or the sparrow-sized black rail seems like a walk in the park.

Both species of tailed frogs are plain brown, with vertical pupils and a variable dark eye stripe. Until recently they were considered to be just one species. Only the male is tailed, and it's actually not a tail but an external part of his cloaca. You tell the two species apart by range: both live in forest-lined torrents, but one is found only in the mountains of Idaho and western Montana, and the other lives in the Pacific Northwest, from Northern California to British Columbia. Look for them along rivers shaded by redwood, spruce, fir, or hemlock, or, less commonly, under deciduous trees like alder and maple.

[opposite] The Rocky Mountain tailed frog can be told from other frogs by size, habitat, and the lack of a round "eardrum" (aka tympanum), that bulging circle behind the eye.

### WHO YOU CALLING PRIMITIVE?

Due to ancestral skeletal features having to do with the particular arrangement of ribs, vertebra, and pelvis shape, the tailed frog is sometimes called primitive. A skeptic might say, "How can you tell—don't all frogs look a bit primitive?" And in rebuttal, an evolutionary

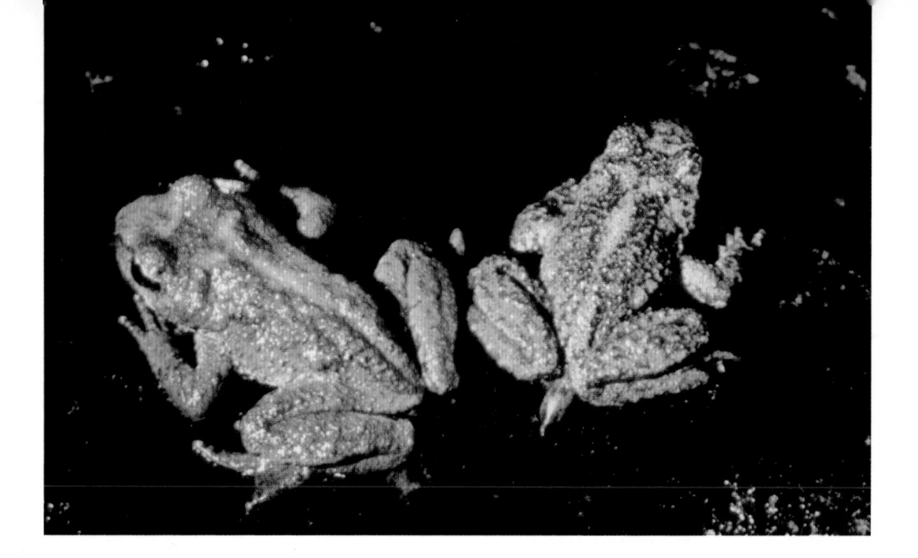

The tailed frog's "tail" is part of a device used in mating.

biologist might add that any given animal comes out of millions of years of trial by fire; no maladapted organism would have made it this far if it wasn't good at survival and reproduction. Everything alive now is field-tested and highly refined.

One interesting adaptation of tailed frogs is how their tadpoles function. Usually you expect tadpoles in warm, still, shallow water. The streams where tailed frogs are found are too cold and fast for other frogs, but their tadpoles have sucker-lipped faces and can cling to the underside of stones, scraping off algal film with their teeth. They do not grow quickly, but they do grow steadily; sources disagree on the specifics, but in general, it seems to take two years or longer for them to mature to adulthood. In contrast, the tadpoles of some toads mature in 14 days (!), though a month or two is more typical. Tailed frog tadpoles have a very good grip, and according to one field guide, they will "hang on to anything solid, including human flesh."

Despite their unique external morphology, tailed frogs mate like most other anurans via amplexus. Female tailed frogs can store viable sperm for up to two years. When finally ready, the large, sticky eggs are deposited in bead-like rows under rocks.

The only thing harder than finding tailed frogs at night is finding their eggs. Birdwatchers who count their orioles, tanagers, and lazuli buntings have no idea how good they have it.

# African clawed frog

*Xenopus laevis*

**FUN FACT**

The trilling call can be repeated 100 times a minute.

| SIZE | FOOD | SPECIES IN OUR AREA |
| --- | --- | --- |
| 2–5 inches | fish, other frogs, invertebrates | 1 |

Like the American bullfrog (page 82), this is another mouth that swims. Why the "clawed" part of the name? It uses its toothed jaws to hold its prey while shredding it with its rear claws and pushing it into its mouth with its front legs.

Color pattern is a basecoat of khaki overlaid with darker green blotches. The authors find all the creatures in this book equally interesting, but compared to other species, a clawed frog's nose looks a little too pointy, the eyes too beady, the legs too pudgy. While it is not a particularly graceful animal, what it does have is perseverance and appetite, and in nature that counts for more than beauty or trim lines.

## FROGS THAT EAT LIKE HOGS

Native to sub-Saharan Africa, the clawed frog in western North America does not have a dedicated predator keen to eat it and only it. But it has the usual range of folks ready to take a shot, as chance allows: herons and egrets mostly, or even the odd owl or raccoon. Feral boars will eat clawed frogs when they can, as will snakes and turtles and largemouth bass. Once an inland reservoir in Orange County was being drained, and it turned out to be chock-a-block with clawed frogs. Since they would die anyway, they were collected by a biological supply service, to be pickled in formaldehyde and used in high school dissection kits.

The frogs in turn need prey to survive, and so the clawed frog can mean bad news for native frog species, especially Pacific treefrogs, red-spotted toads, and western spadefoots. Where freshwater meets the sea in estuaries, clawed frogs can turn to eating marine species, like federally endangered tidewater gobies in Goleta Slough. Yet they can also be highly cannibalistic, so if need arises, they will eat each other.

## VERY EXPENSIVE REAL ESTATE (PLUS AN AIR FORCE BASE)

For now, clawed frogs are firmly established only in Southern California, in the drainages and reservoirs in San Diego, Orange, Los Angeles, and Ventura counties. Of course this is some very expensive property, as well as an area where urbanization, wildland fire, urban runoff, and feral cats put extreme pressure on our native amphibians. Besides bullfrogs and garter snakes and drought and too many people turning over too many streamside stones, oh jeez, now they have to watch out for clawed frogs, too? It does seem unfair. But at least they are not in pupfish drainages

[below left] The African clawed frog is established in the Los Angeles River and elsewhere in Southern California, from San Diego to Ventura.

[below right] In desert wetlands, like Piute Ponds in the Antelope Valley, the frogs have arrived but thankfully can't leave. There is no place to go.

in Death Valley or in Yosemite National Park or the Sacramento Delta. Some in UC Davis and Golden Gate Park were "dealt with" (better not to know the details); scattered records exist in Arizona and Texas.

This voracious frog from Africa can eat its way through an entire river of native frog species.

Clawed frogs can migrate overland on rainy nights, but on average they are dependent on interconnected waterways. At Piute Ponds in the high desert of Edwards Air Force Base (home of the book and movie, *The Right Stuff*), clawed frogs can't go anywhere. It is all Joshua trees and salt pans on all sides. No sane wildlife manager would intentionally release clawed frogs at any new site, but now that they are there, they provide a reliable food source for great blue herons, great egrets, snowy egrets, and black-crowned night herons.

So is this animal coming to a park or stream near you? Unless you're in Southern California, let us hope not.

# spadefoot toads

*Scaphiopus* and *Spea* spp.

FUN FACT

These toads can live for years underground, waiting for the next storm.

| SIZE | FOOD | SPECIES IN OUR AREA |
|---|---|---|
| 1.5–2.5 inches | spiders, beetles, crickets, ants, termites, moths, snails, worms | 5: Couch's spadefoot (*Scaphiopus couchii*), Plains spadefoot (*Spea bombifrons*), western spadefoot (*S. hammondii*), Great Basin spadefoot (*S. intermontana*), Mexican spadefoot (*S. multiplicata*) |

Small and nocturnal, these are coin-sized versions of the toads seen on page 75. They need water to breed but otherwise are land-based. Ours are all cream or tan or olive with light spots or blotches; the female Couch's is especially striking, with a vivid dark-over-green ocelot pattern. All seem a bit pebbly or warty, and the legs often "pull in" to make a compact bundle when not moving.

The common name comes from a tiny black hook on the sole of the back foot, used for digging. The more scientific way to describe that is to say the spadefoot possess "an enlarged, keratinized metatarsal tubercle supported internally by the prehallux."

Pre- or post-hallux, even though spadefoots look like toads, they come from a different part of the evolutionary tree and you can tell them apart by size and by the vertical pupil. You may also notice they don't have the round "eardrum" behind the eye the way bullfrogs or toads do.

Taken as a whole, the spadefoot complex occurs from Canada to Mexico, but the animals themselves can't always be easily found, since they spend months underground. They can survive in quite arid areas; Death Valley does not have spadefoots but Nevada does, and monsoon rains bring them out in Arizona. The western spadefoot is found only in California and northern Baja. Much of its original habitat is now taken up by agriculture and urban development. Vernal pools on the Santa Rosa Plateau, Riverside County, provide one important refuge; this is also a great site for newts and other salamanders, toads, and treefrogs.

## THE BIG SLEEP

Western rains can be hard and brief, and the surface ponds they create may be gone in a few weeks or months. This can be true in the Southwest, with late summer monsoons, as well as California, which usually has only winter rains. In both cases, spadefoots have evolved to exploit the brief gift of water. Basically, they live the same life as any amphibian (egg, tadpole, adult), but fast-forwarded at blazing speed. Eggs can hatch after just a day or two, and tadpoles can be metamorphizing into adults by the two-week mark. This varies by species; some tadpoles need four to 11 weeks to mature.

[opposite] Spadefoots are small desert and grassland toads with vertical pupils.

Once hatched, tadpoles can either be omnivorous, grazing algae or taking what detritus the pond allows, or within the same species, they can be carnivorous. Socially, omnivore-morph tadpoles congregate in groups, while carnivore-morph tadpoles tend to be solitary and to develop more quickly. They may be the same species, but they differ in development and habits; the carnivore tadpoles hunt shrimp but also cannibalize other tadpoles. There are also intergrades, and some of the carnivores later morph back into the plant-grazing body types.

**They can survive many months underground, waiting for the next rainstorm.**

That is it: a brief life in water and then once they become adults, they eat and eat, and then as soon as a month later, they go underground to wait for the next set of storms, even if they have to wait a year. The self-dug burrows are 1–3 feet down and backfilled with soil. While in torpor, the spadefoots avoid drying out by absorbing moisture from the soil. Most go into solitary burrows, though there are reports of sharing, and a few reports of using rodent burrows instead of digging a direct and private foxhole. Desert winters can be brutal, but the soil insulates them and of course while they are that deep they are not being hunted by above-ground foes like coyotes, rattlesnakes, or burrowing owls.

Supercell monsoons leave behind ephemeral pools that are soon filled with calling spadefoots.

Once out on the surface, if confronted by a potential predator, they do secrete toxins, which are sometimes said to give off the smell of roasted peanuts. It is not fatal to humans but can cause a runny nose and red eyes. That means if you handle a spadefoot, wash your hands right away. (This is good advice all the time, and for other species as well.)

When the rains come back, and when the ponds are full and the spadefoots are out and congregating, the male choruses a trilling or quacking call; males and females join up in the water, and the eggs are fertilized as they leave the female. The next generation is ready to carry on. One good thing about using temporary ponds for breeding is that bullfrogs and African clawed frogs don't live in that brief water source, so the tadpoles have a fighting chance.

A spadefoot lives about 10 years, with herp reference estimates ranging from a few years to 13 years.

# chorus frogs and treefrogs

## *Hyla*, *Pseudacris*, and *Smilisca* spp.

FUN FACT

Not all treefrogs live in trees—some burrow like toads.

| SIZE | FOOD | SPECIES IN OUR AREA |
|---|---|---|
| 1–2.5 inches | beetles, moths, spiders, mosquitoes, midges | 9: canyon treefrog (*H. arenicolor*), Arizona treefrog (*H. wrightorum*), California treefrog (*P. cadaverina*), Baja California treefrog (*P. hypochondriaca*), boreal chorus frog (*P. maculata*), Pacific treefrog (*P. regilla*), Sierran treefrog (*P. sierra*), western chorus frog (*P. triseriata*), lowland burrowing treefrog (*S. fodiens*) |

Collectively, these small and often abundant frogs chirrup, yitter, quack, and ribbet—easy to hear, but finding the source is trickier. They blend in well: most are banded or mottled with contrasting hues, but some can be plain green or all-brown. Many have black "bandit masks" through the eyes, a thin dark stripe that carries down onto the shoulder. This helps break up the shape, so they seem like just a shadow of a twig over drab leaves. "Nothing to see here—move along, move along." One cool thing are the feet, especially when seen up close. They have rounded toepads and each digit ends in an itty-bitty golf ball, features that help them shimmy up slick plant stems or cling to vertical granite cliffs. They can even stick to a pane of glass.

The throat of a chorus frog can expand like a balloon when males call for mates.

"You can hear me, but you can't see me"—a Sierran treefrog shows off his camouflage near Sequoia National Park.

## PASS THE BUBBLE YUM GUM

Male frogs calling for mates can be surprisingly loud, and the sound can carry a quarter mile in calm conditions. If you look up a recording of the Pacific treefrog online, you'll probably realize you know their sound already; some days they can seem as incessant as cicadas.

While chorus frogs and treefrogs do call during the day, nighttime is when they really get going. Sound is boosted by expanding throat sacs, which are thin throat membranes that balloon out. If humans had throat sacs—and what a racket, if we did—touching one would feel like pressing a finger against an overinflated surgical glove, and in size, the sac membrane would be larger than a beachball. How exciting it would be to watch a large choir in action, all their throats swelling in unison.

What are the frogs saying? It's dangerous to speculate, but perhaps some version of, "Over here! Pick me, pick me, pick me!" And what do female frogs do? Many female frogs will move around to evaluate multiple callers, waiting until they hear just the right one.

Small size and the racing-stripe mask help distinguish chorus frogs from other toads and frogs.

## A CROWDED DITCH IN IDAHO

Small but common, that is one unifying attribute. In the High Sierra, Pacific treefrogs will be the most common amphibian above 7,000 feet. That same species is also the most common frog in the Northwest, and in Idaho a single pond held 2,000 separate clusters of Pacific treefrog eggs. Treefrogs have been recorded breeding in lakes, ponds, streams, oxbows, swamps, reservoirs, meadows, golf course ponds, and irrigation ditches—if it has water, they try to make it work. Typically, egg laying in all species happens in early to mid-spring, but it can extend deep into summer. In a given wetland, subpopulations of frogs tend to cluster up, probably more an artifact of the call-and-response mating process than microhabitat variation.

During the winter most of these frogs go into a torpor, tucked up in a moist, mossy crevice on a cliff face, or safely burrowed deep in mud. You might still hear some if out hiking, but most of them are waiting for the warmth and abundance of spring.

## TWO, NINE, OR 29 SPECIES?

Again, genus and species boundaries remain in flux in herpetology. Common names vary as well. When it comes to these dapper little frogs, we list nine species for now, but further revision may combine them into fewer units or even subdivide them more finely. For example, some species listed here could wind up in the genus *Hyliola*. The western chorus frog complex in particular could be reorganized; to quote one reviewer, "The entire complex badly needs to be studied using fine scale sampling and nuclear gene sequences."

Who will come along and do the definitive sorting-out? We hope it will be you.

Two colors, one species. Examples of the variability of western chorus frog. Both colors must be equally successful, since both options exist side by side.

# American toads

## *Anaxyrus* and *Incilius* spp.

FUN FACT

Won't give you warts, but their skin can exude toxins.

| SIZE | FOOD | SPECIES IN OUR AREA |
|---|---|---|
| 2–5 inches | frog eggs, crayfish, caterpillars, moths, crickets, snails, beetles, ants | 11: boreal toad (*A. boreas*), arroyo toad (*A. californicus*), Great Plains toad (*A. cognatus*), green toad (*A. debilis*), black toad (*A. exsul*), Arizona toad (*A. microscaphus*), Amargosa toad (*A. nelsoni*), red-spotted toad (*A. punctatus*), Sonoran green toad (*A. retiformis*), Woodhouse toad (*A. woodhousii*), Sonoran desert toad (*I. alvarius*) |

These toads are mostly nocturnal and fist-sized, and when seen at night, they look like a round, compact lump: legs tucked in, eyes shining, skin a blotchy, knobby patchwork of dark over light, sometimes with a thin white line down the middle of the back. Often the front legs prop their bodies up, back legs folded, like a palsied pug trying to sit pretty for a treat. Many field guides still list our toads as genus *Bufo* or *Incilius*, but recent work has reallocated things, and the main American toads are now *Anaxyrus*, "chief of the earth."

Look at the eyes: this Arizona toad does not have the vertical pupils of the spadefoot toads (page 66).

### HOW TO LIVE A LIFETIME IN A MONTH

Toads can live 10 years in the wild, though in some environments, the brevity of the rainy season can mean that they need to practice a stop-start lifestyle. In the Southwest, for example, summer

The black toad is endemic to just one desert valley on the border between California and Nevada.

monsoons trigger a surge of "second spring." The desert kicks into high gear. Hummingbirds swarm the vivid red flowering spikes of chuparosa; Botteri's sparrows sing with a high, sweet trill; butterflies are at their peak abundance; and emerging at night after a year underground, male Woodhouse toads gather around newly formed mud puddles and call *waaaah, waaaah*. Eggs are laid in a long sticky strand, thousands of eggs total, each one about the size of a BB gun pellet. Racing against the pond's inevitable evaporation, tadpoles hatch, graze on pond scum, and in a month or two, get on with Phase 2: growing legs, ditching the tail, getting ready to breathe air, and hopping about and eating insects. At the same time, the new toads and toadlets need to dodge roadrunners, skunks, kestrels, snakes, and just about everything else with quick eyes and a ready mouth.

Once autumn starts to set in, it will be time to find a rodent burrow (or dig a burrow of one's own), going deep before it gets too dry and too cold. Toads are patient: the summer monsoons will be back eventually . . . *they hope*.

## WIDESPREAD YET LOCAL, LOCAL YET MIRACULOUS

The American toads in our region are interesting in that some are restricted to a single valley, like the black toad of Deep Springs, on the California–Nevada border. This is a high steppe ranchland kind of habitat, home to Marlboro men and grand sagebrush vistas. Somehow after the glaciers retreated and the land began to dry out, a relict population of toads got left behind. They have found suitable springs, and thanks to genetic drift, now are their own species, alone in one valley many, many miles from other frogs and toads. They have taken the word *endemic* to a new level.

In contrast, the boreal toad has a range map stretching from Alaska down through Canada and the western United States into the top half of Baja. Depending on altitude and temperature, it might breed as early as January in the desert or as late as July in the High Sierra. It can be found from sea level to above 11,000 feet. It does need water to breed (streams, reservoirs, canals, impoundments) but forages in grasslands, woodlands, meadows, and even the edges of urban parks. It practices what one expert has termed a "flexible biology," as evidenced, for example, by its being one of the first species to appear on deglaciated islands in Glacier Bay National Park.

Isn't that too cold for most cold-blooded animals like amphibians? One might think so, but a stout body and survivalist spirit lets the boreal toad fill newly created ecological niches.

[above] Red-spotted toad, wishing he had brought a bigger coin purse.

[below] Sonoran desert toads are the largest native toad species in the United States.

## LITERATURE'S LONG, LONG REACH

In *Richard III*, Shakespeare's titular character is cursed by prophetic women many times, including being called a "poisonous bunch-backed toad." Toads in Shakespeare are always foul, venomous, and equated with other despised creatures, including adders, bats, beetles, and spiders. Sounds to us like rather good company, and one wonders how much of that Shakespeare really believed versus how much he was vamping up to please his audience. Shakespeare was not trying to make good literature or even bad literature—he was just trying to make a groat or two and live to write another day. If people wanted to hiss and boo and watch the bad guys get called toads, he was happy enough to oblige (and to do it in unrhymed iambic pentameter for three hours straight, to boot).

But this cultural legacy lives on, and even today, some people are a bit afraid of toads. Please don't be: toads are not really going to leave you enthralled by a witch or give you some new variant of the plague. If you pick one up on a nighttime walk, be gentle, wash your hands afterward, and don't be surprised if it pees on you in annoyance or defense.

If a giant UFO swept down out of the night sky and picked you up, you might pee too.

Toads often hunt at night; this California toad (a subspecies of boreal toad) is patrolling an oak woodland.

# red- and yellow-legged frogs

*Rana* spp.

FUN FACT

California red-legged frog is California's state amphibian.

| SIZE | FOOD | SPECIES IN OUR AREA |
|---|---|---|
| 2–3 inches | moths, ants, grasshoppers, beetles, flies, fish, snails | 5: northern red-legged frog (*R. aurora*), foothill yellow-legged frog (*R. boylii*), California red-legged frog (*R. draytonii*), southern mountain yellow-legged frog (*R. muscosa*), Sierra Nevada yellow-legged frog (*R. sierrae*) |

Many adults in this group of small to medium-sized pond frogs do have red (or yellow) legs, and red and yellow sides, too, though it is more like a wash laid down in a watercolor sketch than it is fire engine–saturated or chrome-plated. The brightly colored thighs stay hidden most of the time; when they are used, it is to flash a signal to predators—"I see you, and I can out-hop you." All these species have long legs and narrow waists, with a ridge from neck to hip on each side of the back.

Central habitat is ponds, but also marshes, streams, lagoons, and even a reliably damp willow thicket. Good jumpers but also good to eat, or so early settlers thought; Mark Twain's story about the famous jumping frog of Calaveras County featured the California red-legged frog, though with that species in decline, modern jump-offs now rely on pet bullfrogs. Contrary to the story, nobody is allowed to cheat anymore by filling up a rival's frog with lead shot.

The northern red-legged frog can be found from Mendocino in California north through western Oregon and Washington to southern British Columbia. Foothill yellow-legged frog is in Oregon, California, and Baja. The other species are more exclusively southern: California red-legged frog is in California (coast and Sierra Nevada) and the top end of Baja; Sierra Nevada yellow-legged frog is just in the southern part of that range, and the southern mountain yellow-legged frog is found only in the main inland mountains of Southern California.

The life cycle is typical for frogs: males call to advertise their fitness for mating; the male and female frogs join in amplexus; eggs are laid in the water; the eggs hatch as tadpoles; in time, the tadpoles become frogs.

This group has faced challenges, and, sadly, many populations have declined. Everything seems stacked against them, and issues include pesticide accumulation, the introduction of non-native trout (including native trout raised in hatcheries and introduced to previously trout-free streams), urbanization, fires, and the same chytrid fungus that harms so many other amphibians.

Of the species in this grouping, the northern red-legged frog may be in the best shape. For the California red-legged frog, many different reintroduction and transplantation projects have been carried out, but with mixed results. Fire and drought complicate reintroduction, and some possible impediments, like the presence of non-native bullfrogs, can be assumed to be a problem, but so far the direct threat from bullfrogs has not been conclusively studied.

**The Sierra Nevada yellow-legged frog can thrive at sites all the way to 12,000 feet and was native to streams like this one. Endangered now, its decline is blamed in part on introduced trout.**

## NATURE SANCTUARIES VS. NATURE REALITIES

We want this book to be honest but encouraging, and with this group of frogs, even the ones on endangered species

lists, all is not hopeless. In the case of the California red-legged frog, in Marin County alone there are 120 breeding sites, "with a total adult population of several thousand frogs." Where are they all? Perhaps concentrated inside Muir Woods National Monument, or behind a tall fence at a special Save the Frogs nature sanctuary? No—they are just making do with the options available, and that includes pastures and rangeland. One survey found that for the Marin County red-legged frogs, "most of these sites are artificial stock ponds constructed on lands that have been grazed by cattle for 150 years."

**The California red-legged frog was declared the state's official amphibian in 2014. Mark Twain wrote about this species.**

From the western fence lizards you might see in your backyard to chuckwallas in Phoenix to the salamanders thriving in Berkeley's Tilden Park, reptiles and amphibians are all around us. And there are opportunities for everybody to enjoy them and to participate in helping, from doing follow-up counts at reintroduction sites to posting your own phone shots to sites like iNaturalist or HerpMapper when you do find something good. Not sure if you have a red-legged frog or something more common? Post it and find out.

# American bullfrog

## *Rana catesbeiana*

FUN FACT

The usual call of this largest American frog is *jug-o-rum*, but when captured, they can give a sharp scream (presumably to startle the heron into letting go).

| SIZE | FOOD | SPECIES IN OUR AREA |
| --- | --- | --- |
| 3–8 inches | fish, crayfish, snakes, other frogs: anything it can catch | 1 |

Bullfrogs *look* like frogs: broad face, long legs, pond-edge habits. They can be green, brown, or black, mostly plain or with bands of darker splotches. This is a sit-and-wait predator; you might walk right by one and not notice until the splash lets you know it has jumped into deeper water for hiding.

A frog that looks like a frog, the bullfrog is introduced in the West but native elsewhere in North America.

The American bullfrog is native to the eastern half of the continent, but introduced populations now occur from the Salton Sea to the Canadian border; as a habitat and appetite generalist,

Bullfrogs manage to survive everywhere, even the shallow, saline Salton Sea.

it adapts to just about any wet, reedy place. It's a frequent part of the summer nighttime chorus—or it is if you live near a lake, a marsh, a creek, or even a sewage pond in the middle of the desert. Both sexes look similar, but you can tell them apart by the diameter of the tympanum (that bulging circle behind the eye)—larger than the eye means it is a male; same size or smaller, a female. The males defend territory with their baritone call, which can be heard up to a quarter mile away.

If the male's calling works, the resulting eggs (in the words of poet Jim Dodge) are an "amalgam of electric jelly." More prosaically, the eggs float at the surface in a disk an inch thick and a few inches wide; up to 20,000 eggs can comprise one mass. Those hatch into tadpoles that mostly graze plants but sometimes take small insects. Tadpoles themselves can be a whopping 6 inches—larger than adults of most other species.

## TOO MUCH MOUTH, NOT ENOUGH HEART

In "Joy to the World," Three Dog Night sang about Jeremiah, who was a bullfrog. Catchy tempo, but not everybody is a fan. Here is a description from Virginia, 1705: "In the Swamps and running Streams, they have Frogs of an incredible bigness, which are called Bull-frogs, from the roaring they make." By 1905 these bellowing, bull-necked amphibians were present in California. Most biologists wish they had never come. The problem is the mouth: a whole lot can fit in it, and these animals do not discriminate between the good, the bad, or the ugly. Searching the internet turns up shots of bullfrogs eating everything from goldfish to finches to bats to other bullfrogs. In that voracious gulping down of all that swims, wiggles, hops, or scuttles, bullfrogs can inexorably eat all the native frogs in a given waterway.

Once bullfrogs become established, not much slows down their spread except truly ephemeral conditions. Unlike native desert toads and frogs, the bullfrog needs access to continuous water in order to survive; it can't burrow into the drying mud and wait for next summer the way a red-legged frog or a spadefoot toad can.

Tadpoles are sometimes called pollywogs; the two names mean the same thing—the aquatic stage between egg and adulthood.

A green heron makes a lucky jab at a metamorph, when a frog is part tadpole, part adult.

### TASTES LIKE CHICKEN

Almost all restaurant frog legs—in French, *cuisses de grenouille*—come from this species, which is one way they've gotten to be so many places they don't belong, including five countries in Europe as well as Thailand, Mexico, and most of Japan. These frogs weren't all escapees from food farms; some were released pets. Should we say it again? *Never do this*. Supposedly the meat tastes like chicken, in a stringy, fishy, bland sort of way, and the overall shape and meat-to-bone ratio recalls chicken wings.

Hunting wild bullfrogs (aka frog gigging) requires a flashlight and a small trident, spear, or knife on a pole. Since this is a pest species in the American West, gig on.

# leopard frogs

*Rana* spp.

FUN FACT

A leopard frog once caught and ate a bat.

| SIZE | FOOD | SPECIES IN OUR AREA |
| --- | --- | --- |
| 3.5–5 inches | insects, snails, leeches, fish, other frogs | 9: Rio Grande leopard frog (*R. berlandieri*), Plains leopard frog (*R. blairi*), Chiricahua leopard frog (*R. chiricahuensis*), relict leopard frog (*R. onca*), northern leopard frog (*R. pipiens*), southern leopard frog (*R. sphenocephala*), wood frog (*R. sylvatica*), Tarahumara frog (*R. tarahumarae*), lowland leopard frog (*R. yavapaiensis*) |

Midsized and agile, leopard frogs take their name from dark spots that flow down a green, tan, or olive back. Two raised ridges down each side of the back make a thin racing stripe that runs from ear to hip. These are often water-centric frogs, found in seeps, ponds, streams, canals, and stock tanks from sea level to above 10,000 feet; they forage away from water too, especially in meadows or thicker grasses, but not in open areas like rangeland or mowed lawns.

Unlike some other toads and frogs, the skin does not exude toxic slime. If there's danger, the leopard frog hopes to use speed to get away.

## *PHANTOM OF THE OPERA* FROG

In *The Phantom of the Opera*, the vain diva Carlotta is cursed by the Phantom, and her singing voice comes out as a frog's croak. It sounds comically harsh and discordant to us but might work fine in an all-frog opera. One handbook says that the Chiricahua leopard frog "rapidly pulses snores" interspersed with grunts and "chuckles." Rio Grande leopard frog—introduced into Arizona during the establishment of warm-water game fish from Texas—makes "short squawks," reminiscent of "the sound of a finger quickly stroking an inflated balloon." Plains leopard frog, found in southeastern Arizona, New Mexico, and further east, has vocalizations that include grunting, grinding, and kissing.

Usually these calls are given at night. They help males claim territory and attract mates, the same as the songs and wing-rubbings of birds and cicadas, the same as the hooting of gibbons or the hours-long serenade of humpback whales.

## ENDEMICS VS. GENERALISTS

Like other amphibians, leopard frogs are vulnerable to habitat loss, habitat fragmentation, drought, chytrid fungus, and predation by non-native frogs and fish, but in addition some have limited ranges as well.

[opposite] Leopard frogs are so called for their spots.

The Chiricahua leopard frog takes its name from a sky island mountain range in southeastern Arizona that is famous among birdwatchers; the area is also home to Chiricahua National Monument and a biology research center (and, in some years, to jaguars that have wandered north out of Mexico). The species had become alarmingly rare, but recent conservation and reintroduction efforts are helping to restore it. The Phoenix Zoo is one of the lead partners, and since 1995, using a core of captive breeding frogs, it has released over 25,000 Chiricahua leopard frog tadpoles, juveniles, and adults back into the wild.

This frog species may be not one but two; another population that occurs farther north along the Mogollon Rim is a strong candidate for being split into its own species. A species with a singular range in one unit (a particular mountain or state) is said to be endemic to that region. That might be a salamander or a lily—or a frog.

The other approach is to be widespread and generalized, the way a ponderosa pine, western bluebird, or (in the leopard frog family) the northern leopard frog is. Its range in our area includes all the western states and south from New Mexico into Mexico. In some places where it was native (such as in California east of the Sierra), it is no longer found; in other places, like at Lake Tahoe or

The circle just behind the eye is the tympanum, a membrane that passes sound to a frog's ears.

in Los Angeles, it now occurs because it was introduced intentionally as a food source or else because captive individuals intended to be dissected in biology classes escaped. The northern leopard frog's extensive range also includes Canada and the top half of the United States. It is the state amphibian of Minnesota and Vermont—long may it rattle and rave.

Typical habitat of the imperiled Chiricahua leopard frog, which is limited to two disjunct ranges in southeastern Arizona, western New Mexico, and northern Sonora.

## THREE HERPETOLOGISTS WALK INTO A BAR

We list leopard frogs as genus *Lithobates* ("rock climber"). Other sources still put them in the earlier catchall genus *Rana*, a worldwide group that can include up to 150 species, ranging from the Tsushima brown frog, endemic to one island in Japan, to the Italian stream frog, found in Italy and San Marino. People get surprisingly testy when defending their choices. Who is right? Maybe none of us: more research may reallocate some of these to a third, as-yet-unknown genus. Science never ends—it is the hit Broadway musical that will have an infinite run, and there are many Sunday matinees yet to come.

# REPTILES

# sea turtles

*Caretta*, *Chelonia*, *Dermochelys*, and *Lepidochelys* spp.

**FUN FACT**

Sea turtles weigh 100–400 pounds; the record is 540 pounds.

| SIZE | FOOD | SPECIES IN OUR AREA |
| --- | --- | --- |
| 3–4 feet | omnivorous when young; mostly plants in adulthood (green sea turtles) | 4: loggerhead sea turtle (*Caretta caretta*), green sea turtle (*Chelonia mydas*), leatherback sea turtle (*D. coriacea*), olive ridley sea turtle (*L. olivacea*) |

Welcome to the group of reptiles that turns everything upside-down. While a desert tortoise plods along at a deliberate .13 miles an hour, a swimming sea turtle can outpace a sprinter trying to keep up on the shore. Yet if it is resting, a sea turtle needs to come up to the surface to breathe only every four to seven hours. Some individuals may be over 100 years old, and a few are big—*really* big: record-setting leatherbacks can be 9 feet long and weigh more than a car. Worldwide, there are six or seven species, but only one, the green sea turtle, is easily seen in our area, and that is the one we focus on here.

## TAKE ME TO YOUR LEADER

All sea turtles share a similar body plan: each one is a flying saucer-shaped disk with blade-shaped flippers. Instead of teeth, they have hooked mouths that resemble parrot beaks. They row or scull in the water, doing the breast stroke with their front flippers. The back feet mostly function as rudders. There is a small tail, but unlike those of whales and fish, a sea turtle's tail doesn't help move it around. Most sea turtle shells are brown or tortoiseshell; the green sea turtle's common name refers not to its shell but to the greenish fat revealed when sailors killed it for food.

All sea turtles lay their eggs on tropical beaches, usually the same ones they were born on. In California, the resident green sea turtles nest in Mexico and are slowly increasing in number. Playa Colola is one well-studied nesting site, and over 1,000 turtles were seen laying eggs in one night. Other than egg-laying, sea turtles spend their lives swimming in the sea; they can drink seawater, exuding the processed salt from glands near their eyes.

Worldwide, many adult sea turtles eat jellyfish and so are at risk from plastic bags and other marine trash that looks like jellies. The adult green sea turtle is the exception to the trend. While it can drown in abandoned fishing nets or be hit by speeding boats, it does not eat jellyfish and instead grazes on undersea grasses (and that's probably where the green color comes from). Following warm water currents north, green sea turtles, like all the Pacific Coast sea turtles, can be seen in Oregon and Washington, and even stray as far north as Alaska.

**[opposite] Sea turtles breathe air and can be seen when they come to the surface.**

## WRINKLEBUTTS AND POWER PLANTS

[above left] In Southern California, sea turtles congregate at the warm water outflows from power plants.

[above right] The green sea turtle likes warm, shallow bays and lagoons, where rich nutrients and ample sunlight help the plants it eats flourish.

To see a sea turtle on the Pacific Coast, four options rise to the top of the list. Seabird study trips and whalewatching boats based in Monterey sometimes see the jellyfish-eating species, like leatherbacks. A second choice is San Diego Bay: at least 60 green sea turtles are year-round residents in the south end of the bay, including one the researchers call Wrinklebutt. (In trade, what does it call each researcher? "Oh look, here comes Pointy Nose, followed by his sunburned friend, Pink Foot.") A third choice is La Jolla Cove, just to the north, where a sea turtle subgroup lives.

The fourth choice is Anaheim Bay in Southern California. Here at the border of Orange and Los Angeles counties, the San Gabriel River reaches the sea. Power plants use seawater for cooling, and when the water flows back into the river, it comes out warmer than when it came in. Seagrasses like that and so do the cold-blooded green sea turtles. Taking a bike ride upstream along the paved bike path is a great way to look for them.

Native Americans captured wild sea turtles for food, but that was seemingly a rare source of sustenance for them, based on how few turtle remains we've found. As attitudes toward protecting marine resources change (and as sea temperatures rise), will sea turtle populations expand north? Black skimmers and other tropical seabirds now turn up in places they were never seen previously, and in warm-water years, brown boobies head north from Mexico and take up residence. Will sea turtles follow?

The killer whales of Puget Sound certainly hope so.

# western pond turtle

*Actinemys marmorata*

**FUN FACT**

If ponds dry up, this turtle can survive on dry land for 200 days.

| SIZE | FOOD | SPECIES IN OUR AREA |
|---|---|---|
| 4–8 inches | insects, fish, crayfish, plants | 1 |

Once upon a time, this was *the* west coast turtle, found along the Pacific Coast from Puget Sound to Baja and, especially in the great Central Valley of California, once numbering in the millions. It was the most common pond turtle west of the Sierras.

Note the past tense—this all *was* true, once. What happened to them?

The Gold Rush, that was one thing, and when all those hungry and newly arrived miners needed dinner, nobody did an environmental impact report before making vat after vat of turtle soup. Indeed, in San Francisco in the 1850s, one might have a breakfast omelet made from seabird eggs collected on the Farallon Islands, turtle soup for lunch, and salmon with oysters for dinner, perhaps with a side of venison and a broth made from cattails and native watercress. Wash it all down with some premium California wines—which at the time came exclusively from Los Angeles.

Another, later factor in reducing the western pond turtle's range was agricultural conversion: the tule marshes of California's Central Valley were drained to become cotton and almonds and feedlots and cantaloupes. You can't grow chardonnay in a swamp.

Western pond turtles look like the red-eared slider (left) but have plain faces and smooth (not lightly scalloped) shell edges.

Indigenous populations sustainably harvested this self-contained food as well; once dispatched, it could be roasted right in the shell.

Given the central role of the western pond turtle in feeding so many native and newly arrived people, perhaps the turtle, not the grizzly bear, should have been memorialized on the California state flag.

## A DAY IN THE LIFE OF A COLD-BLOODED ANIMAL

Go to any lake or park today, and the turtle basking on the rock is usually not this one, but the non-native red-eared slider (see next entry). The western pond turtle is the *other* one—still common in some places, but plain-faced and long-tailed and oval-shelled. Both turtles look muddy green (muddier and greener some days more than others), but the native species has a plain cheek, and the introduced species is the one with a red blaze along the side of the face.

There are also a few introduced snapping turtles in our region, imports from the South with a mean head and a tenacious bite, and a second kind of common, non-native turtle, the western painted turtle, which is discussed in the red-eared slider entry.

Pond turtles forage aquatically by preference, though as ponds dry up, they can move into grassland, ditches, or even oak woodland, either to wait out the dry season in a nest or to carry on life in a new waterway. In a typical pond on a typical day, they will bask mid-morning into the afternoon, letting the sun bring core body temperature up as high as the mid-80s Fahrenheit before they sink back down into the dark and cool depths of a pond or river to continue foraging. (They also can tolerate coastal lagoons and brackish water.)

Hunting or grazing in a deep pond, their body temperature may slowly drop to the mid-60s, until it nearly matches the water's ambient temperature. Time then to climb back out onto a fallen log or embankment or even floating vegetation, to soak up more sunlight and warm a chilled core back up again.

Turtles evolved their current body plans over 200 million years ago. Looking at them today, it is not hard to imagine them being good for another 200 million.

**Classic turtle habitat, especially when there are logs and stones to bask on.**

# red-eared slider

## *Trachemys scripta*

**FUN FACT**

When the female is digging a nest chamber, she softens the dirt with urine.

| SIZE | FOOD | SPECIES IN OUR AREA |
| --- | --- | --- |
| 6–12 inches, occasionally larger | plants, insects, shrimp, snails, crayfish, carrion | 1 |

This attractive but non-native (to our region) pond turtle has the dubious distinction of being the only animal in the book to have made it onto a Top 100 list. Which list is that? Thanks to the pet trade and thoughtless humans, the red-eared slider is listed as one of the world's worst invasive species. According to the California Department of Fish and Wildlife, "More than 52 million individual sliders were exported from the United States to international markets between 1989 and 1997." From Australia to Walla Walla, sliders mean bad news.

How did it happen? Native originally to the lower Midwest, lower Mississippi River basin, and the Gulf Coast drainages, red-eared sliders are attractive and durable, and so entered the pet trade early. The usual pattern is that a family gets a pet turtle for the kids, but the turtle grows and the kids' interest doesn't, and in a misguided attempt to solve the problem, the now ex-pet is chucked into the nearest park, pond, ditch, or reservoir, along with a few goldfish, carp, or New Zealand mudsnails to keep it company.

Yellow stripes and a red "ear" are typical face markings. Older red-eared sliders often look plainer.

Red-eared sliders are especially fecund, and if released, and if they find mates (and they usually do), then they compete with native species for food, egg-laying sites, and basking logs. They also spread disease and parasites. Of course, we've heard this story before: see for example American bullfrog (page 82).

## HOW TO RECOGNIZE A SLIDER

Turtle identification is tricky but not impossible. With this species, beware of color variations; while some older red-eared sliders get fairly dark and plain, most sliders show yellow doodles on the face and separate plates of the shell, plus a prominent red racing stripe behind the eye. They also tend to be seen in more urban areas, and if you can see the front feet, they usually have long, visible claws. The western pond turtle (page 95) has a long tail and no fancy markings on face or shell. The western painted turtle (*Chrysemys picta*), another common, non-native turtle, has yellow face scribbles but no red ear patch.

Why "sliders"? It's either because (a) if they sense trouble, they slide off a log into the water as easily as if they are riding on oiled skids, or else (b) because the young ones, when gobbled up by herons and egrets, slide down the bird's gullet with a quick toss of the head. (Hint: pick A.)

## RUNNING THE NUMBERS

A common expression for exponential growth is "breeding like rabbits." The reason red-eared sliders get such a bad rap is that this species beats any amorous lagomorph: females are able to lay up to six clutches per year, each containing up to 30 eggs. That potentially adds 180 new sliders in one pond in one year, and if each of the 180 survives and has 180 viable eggs, that comes out to 32,400 by the end of year two. Not all clutches will be so large, of course, and some hatchlings will die or become sliders for herons and catfish. But many will survive, and with numbers accumulating like that, no native turtle can keep up.

A small fountain makes this island attractive, but all these sliders just want to get warm in the sunshine.

The yellow stripes often extend onto the legs.

Where do they live? (Besides pet stores and toilet bowls, that is.) If there are people and ponds with public access, there are probably red-eared sliders. A very abbreviated list would include Seattle, Portland, Eugene, Bend, Spokane, Boise, Salt Lake City, Reno, Bishop, Las Vegas, Flagstaff, Phoenix, Tucson, Nogales—red-eared sliders are present in all those places and in at least 20 of California's 58 counties, as well as saturating the entire coastal slope from Goleta to Tijuana. So far, there are no records for the center of Death Valley, the summit of Mount Whitney, or the near side of the Moon, but that doesn't mean they're not coming soon.

None of this is the turtles' fault. Whenever an ecosystem has a problem with invasive species knocking checks and balances all to heck, usually there is a guilty bipedal primate lurking somewhere very close by.

# desert tortoises

*Gopherus* spp.

**FUN FACT**

Mojave desert tortoise is the state reptile of both California and Nevada.

| SIZE | FOOD | SPECIES IN OUR AREA |
| --- | --- | --- |
| 9–15 inches | plants (grass, flowers, buds, cactus fruit) | 2: Mojave desert tortoise (*G. agassizii*), Sonoran desert tortoise (*G. morafkai*) |

It seems like an ancient riddle: what lives in a cave, has the legs of an elephant, and is the color of an Army tank left out in the sun too long? And whatever the answer is, we need to make sure the answer has room for a long-lost twin, since recently the "only child" desert tortoise was split into two species.

The Mojave desert tortoise breeds in spring and lives in the southeastern deserts of California, the bottom fifth of Nevada, and adjacent corners of southern Utah and northwestern Arizona. Looking just like it (but breeding in monsoonal summer and fall), the Sonoran desert tortoise fills out the left half of a map of Arizona and extends south into Mexico.

Four additional species occur in Sinaloa, Texas, the Chihuahuan Desert, and the American Southeast. Pet tortoises (which are sometimes illegally released into the wild—*never do this*) can be hybrids involving all six species.

## THANKS, BUT I USED THE RESTROOM LAST MONTH

In the desert, life is seen in essential clarity, as austere beauty juxtaposes against the basic necessities of organizing food, water, and shelter. The desert tortoise solves each of these challenges in a different way. For food, they are able to eat a large variety of plants—some surveys say 20 or 30 species, and others document twice as many as that. Generalist vegetarians usually have the most options in any given ecozone.

Good advice—for this species and all the others.

Water is where tortoises really have it figured out. If it rains, of course they will drink. But nice as water is, they can do without, getting it from their food and storing water internally in their bladder for 200 or even 300 days in a row. They tolerate levels of uric acid in their blood that would kill a human many times over, and when they do "pee," it is a smear of thin, white paste. In some instances, they even have been observed scraping out a "catchment basin" to store rainwater, creating a mini-impoundment that can hold runoff for up to six hours.

Slow and
steady wins the
race (just as
Aesop told us).

To survive extremes, one needs the right kind of under-the-earth shelter, of course. Desert tortoise burrows have an oval opening, so are usually easy to spot. (Badgers can create dens that shape too but usually have more vigorous dirt fans, and, sometimes, a dirt-plug door.) Their tunnels, which can extend 10 feet down, are cool in summer and warm in winter. Tortoises usually hibernate from October to March, though dates vary by location, by wet year or dry year, and maybe just by the mood of the individual reptile in question. During spring and summer, the burrow is used for midday siestas, though less-ideal spots under a creosote bush or shady rock get used too.

## I (DON'T) HEART RAVENS

How long does a typical desert tortoise live? We don't know all the details yet, but published sources give a range of 30 to 60 years.

The trick is making it past the first few years. When first hatched, a desert tortoise has a thin shell and is just 3 inches long. What wants to eat them would be a fair question and the answer would be, "More or less, everything." And *everything* includes Gila monsters, coachwhip snakes, roadrunners, red-tailed hawks, golden eagles, kit foxes, bobcats, spotted skunks, coyotes, badgers, ringtails, pumas, jaguars, and feral dogs. Lucky for baby tortoises that dolphins don't live in the desert or Flipper might go after them as well.

But of all these threats and enemies and hungry mouths, the baddest of black-hatted bad guys is *Corvus corax*, the common raven. They were always around—this is a native desert species, as native as the Joshua tree and the cactus wren—but roadkill, landfills, fast-food parking lots, and back porches with open bowls of dog and kitty kibble, plus an abundance of human-supplied nesting platforms in the form of billboards and telephone poles, all have combined to skew raven populations abnormally high. Ravens need water, but what with irrigation canals, leaky pipes, and sewage ponds, we provide that too.

A conservative estimate is that the raven population in the western Mojave has increased more than sevenfold in the last 25 years. And one kind of food that ravens like even better than

day-old French fries is baby tortoises. Ravens can behead them or just bash a hole in the shell with their pole-axe beaks. A single raven nest accumulated a pile of 250 tortoise shells underneath it over a four-year span.

This level of predation distresses land managers and nature lovers alike. Lasers, drones, shotguns, decoy turtle shells filled with noxious oil—scientists have tried everything possible to deter ravens and save tortoises. Which one is the right answer? So far, there isn't one.

[above left] Anybody home? Desert tortoises often dig burrows with a wide, oval entrance, like this one.

[above right] Scutes, the puzzle pieces on a tortoise's shell, are made of keratin, like fingernails, pangolin scales, and rhino horns. This old shell was found in the Mojave Desert.

## WHAT YOU CAN DO

Captive tortoises, no matter what their origin, should not be returned to the desert. There is too much risk of introducing diseases the wild tortoises are not ready to handle, even if it is the right species for that area. And mind your rubbish, please—don't inadvertently feed more crows, ravens, and roof rats. Last, wild tortoises should not be picked up, since the stress may make them pee, and pee a *lot*, and in drought years, they can't recover the lost water.

Where to go to look for one? There are plenty of nature reserves, national parks, and tortoise conservation areas all over the American desert, and on any hike you take, even if you don't find a desert tortoise, there are a thousand other pleasures to investigate instead.

# western banded gecko

*Coleonyx variegatus*

FUN FACT

Lizards in this genus are our only native geckos.

| SIZE | FOOD | SPECIES IN OUR AREA |
|---|---|---|
| 2–3 inches, plus a tail of 1–2 inches | small invertebrates | 1 |

[left] Geckos store fat in their tails—the fatter the tail, the healthier the lizard.

[opposite, top] Banded geckos are nocturnal and can often be found traversing rocky washes.

[opposite, bottom] In some cultures, geckos are feared as "venomous." Rest assured that they are not; actually, they are gentle creatures and should be handled with care.

Geckos are unlike any other lizards in the West—with their soft skin, skinny toes, and slow gait, these lizards may appear delicate but can live in some extreme environments. The western banded gecko can be identified by its small scales, vertical pupils, and moveable eyelids. True geckos in the family Gekkonidae lack eyelids and lick their eyes to keep them clean. In contrast, the western banded gecko and its relatives belong to the family Eublepharidae, or eye-lidded geckos. They have thick tails that become increasingly thin toward the tip and the body is banded, though the pattern is highly variable across the range. The thickness of the tail usually indicates whether the lizard is eating well or not. The tails are very fragile and can break easily, so take extra care not to startle these lizards if you see one. The tail can regenerate, but that costs the wee creature a fair amount of metabolic capital.

This is a wide-ranging species that encompasses the entire Baja peninsula, Southern California and very southern Nevada, western Arizona, and southern New Mexico, as well as Texas along the Rio Grande. They prefer desert scrub habitat but can also be found along rocky slopes where they use rocks as shelter from daytime temperatures. In the spring and summer, females may lay one or more clutches of one or two eggs.

**Banded geckos have some variation in pattern, but our species is true to the common name for the genus.**

These lizards are nocturnal, and they hunt on the ground for spiders and insects during the night. To see one, slow and steady is the name of the game. Try walking or driving, again *slowly*, along quiet roads at night in the summer. Sandy washes or patches of desert scrub near dirt roads are also good places to look.

If you find a western banded gecko, you may notice its unique, almost cat-like posture: an arched back and upturned tail is the gecko's way of signaling to predators that they have been spotted. The curled tail is also thought to mimic a scorpion's stinger. The gecko may also emit a high-pitched *squeak* if startled.

We do not want to anthropomorphize, but as the photos show, one common reaction when seeing a wild gecko is to say "How cute!" The next is to reach for your phone, to get a picture. Both reactions are valid and normal. Don't forget to upload to iNaturalist or HerpMapper afterward.

# Gila monster

## *Heloderma suspectum*

**FUN FACT**
The tail stores enough fat for this lizard to survive a full year.

| SIZE | FOOD | SPECIES IN OUR AREA |
|---|---|---|
| 18–24 inches including tail | reptile eggs, bird eggs, other lizards, mammals, carrion | 1 |

The genus name *Heloderma* (Greek for "studded skin") refers to the bumpy appearance of its members' skins; the skin's texture is created by the presence of osteoderms, small bony deposits that function like built-in armor. Gila is a river in Arizona, and in addition to this monster, the word is applied to a national forest, a trout, a woodpecker, a krautrock band, and a Native American community. A Gila monster can often be seen flicking a dark, forked tongue to "smell" its prey, the way snakes do, using the Jacobson's organ.

This is a large lizard, with a body over a foot long and a long, thick tail. Unlike many other lizards of the Southwest, the Gila monster's tail will not regenerate if broken. The thick tail stores fat. As with the banded gecko, the fatter the tail, the healthier the lizard. These animals are easily recognizable by orange or pink splotches over a black base, a color pattern whose basic message to predators is, "I'm venomous! Don't even try it." Besides a big head and the implied menace of a venomous bite, for some hikers, the Gila monster's slow, lumbering gait contributes to its monster-like appearance.

## PASS THE EGGS

Gila monsters can be found in southeastern California, southern Nevada, and southwestern Utah; they also occur in Arizona and northern Mexico. They prefer desert scrub and semi-desert grasslands, being especially partial to rocky canyons and areas with enough rocks for cover.

Reptile and bird eggs are typical meals, though they will also eat small mammals. They forage widely (more often at night, in summer) and often return to the same sheltering rock afterward. If there were a Top 10 list for critters in this book that people want to see in person, this one almost certainly is on it. Yet they can be hard to track down, even for trained herpetologists. Good places to try in Arizona include Sabino Canyon and the foothills of the Chiricahua and Santa Catalina Mountains. They may be slightly more active (or at least more often above ground) in spring. If you have a special go-to spot for this species, be sure to let us know.

Please note that this is a protected species: it is illegal to handle, capture, or kill a Gila monster anywhere in the United States and Mexico.

[above] Sabino Canyon near Tucson is lovely even if you don't come across a resident Gila monster.

[opposite, top] Gila monsters move across the ground in a slow, lumbering manner.

[opposite, bottom] Bony deposits in its skin give the Gila monster a "beaded" appearance.

## VENOM: GOOD FOR DEFENSE, GOOD FOR RESEARCH

The Gila monster's venom is delivered through grooved teeth on the lower jaw, and the venom slides along the groove and into the victim like water down a slide. Bites are reportedly extremely painful, resulting in swelling and possible drops in blood pressure. Because these lizards are quite slow walkers, venom is critical for defense against coyotes, foxes, raptors, and other predators.

It also means that the Gila monster is very unlikely to catch up to a hiker and inflict a bite. Most human bites come from mishandling, and they are rare: the last bite that resulted in a human death was in 1930. Many of the peptides in Gila monster venom have inspired medical research. Perhaps the best known is exendin-4, which mediates glucose uptake and insulin release after meals and is therefore used to help people with type 2 diabetes.

**As if the strong jaws, venomous bite, and bright colors weren't enough to make you avoid touching a Gila monster, they are also a protected species.**

## WHEN IN MEXICO . . .

You are unlikely to confuse the Gila monster with any other lizards in its range, except possibly the chuckwalla (page 128), which is somewhat similar in coloration but lacks the bony scale deposits and has a much longer tail. The Gila monster has only one other close relative, the Mexican beaded lizard, which looks similar but, as the name suggests, occurs only in Mexico (and Guatemala).

# legless lizards

## *Anniella* spp.

**FUN FACT**

The legless lizards represent one of the many instances of leg reduction in reptiles.

| SIZE | FOOD | SPECIES IN OUR AREA |
|---|---|---|
| 4–7 inches; with tail, about 9 inches | insects, insect larvae, other arthropods | 5: temblor legless lizard (*A. alexanderae*), Southern Sierra legless lizard (*A. campi*), Bakersfield legless lizard (*A. grinnelli*), northern legless lizard (*A. pulchra*), San Diegan legless lizard (*A. stebbinsi*) |

The California legless lizards are medium-sized, snake-shaped, limbless, burrowing species that once were believed to be a single species, but recent studies have reorganized them into at least five. All species inhabit coastal and sandy areas with some plant cover along the Pacific Coast from San Francisco Bay down to northern Baja. Besides coastal areas, they also occur inland on slopes of the Central Valley and in the Tehachapi Mountains at elevations up to 6,000 feet. These secretive species require loose soil to burrow into and relatively higher humidity environments than most other lizards in this book. Moisture too is essential for shedding their skin, which otherwise will accumulate, obstructing their movements and hunting.

Legless lizards have a cylindrical, elongated body, with a mostly indistinct neck and blunt tail. Skin is smooth and shiny, usually with a dark silvery or dark blue dorsal color and brighter yellow or whitish bellies. A dorsal and two lateral stripes are usually visible. However, those in coastal sand dunes around Monterey Bay occur in brown and black forms, and other populations have very faint or absent striping. Females and males are difficult identify, despite males usually being smaller than females. Two to four young are born between September and November. Young individuals look just like miniaturized versions of their parents, with the same color pattern.

A legless lizard forages using its shovel-shaped snout to make its way through loose earth, feeding primarily on beetles, termites, ants, insect larvae, and other arthropods, like spiders. They are also prey of other reptiles, like ring-necked snakes, and many birds. If threatened, legless lizards can detach their tails to confuse predators and attempt escape.

## WINK-WINK

Legless lizards are not snakes. Unlike snakes, they have two lungs that are equal in size—and eyelids; if you inspect them closely, you will see them blink. Look for these incredible animals by flipping logs and wood boards in sandy areas. They will remain motionless under the sand, so you can use a small stick to gently

Most populations of legless lizards are in coastal dunes, but they can also be found inland around rocky outcrops, such as Vasquez Rocks near Los Angeles.

[above left] Often staying hidden under the sand or dirt, legless lizards can be a challenge to spot.

[above right] Legless lizards resemble small, blunt-tailed snakes.

rake the floor and uncover them. Legless lizards do not bask directly in the sun and can remain active in cool weather, being most active in the morning and late afternoon.

Just as with many other species of small reptiles and amphibians, habitat destruction due human development is the main threat. Legless lizards are listed as species of special concern by the California Department of Fish and Wildlife and as sensitive species by the United States Forest Service, but the exact boundaries of their ranges are still being worked out, making your potential contributions of new records in HerpMapper or iNaturalist even more important.

# alligator lizards

## *Elgaria* spp.

**FUN FACT**

Three more species live in Mexico.

| SIZE | FOOD | SPECIES IN OUR AREA |
|---|---|---|
| 4–8 inches, plus a tail up to twice as long | insects, slugs, other lizards | 4: northern alligator lizard (*E. coerulea*), Madrean alligator lizard (*E. kingii*), southern alligator lizard (*E. multicarinata*), Panamint alligator lizard (*E. panamintina*) |

Four species but one set of blueprints. Alligator lizard "base model" is a slim, brown, 4- to 8-inch lizard with a tail up to twice as long as the body. The legs quote T-rex and seem too small for the torso, as if they were borrowed from somebody else. Many people comment on how snake-like these lizards are when they move, sometimes even dragging themselves forward using only the front legs. The snaky aspect is further reinforced by an easily detached tail, so a potential predator will be distracted by the tail's still-wiggling presence while the main animal gets away. Pick one up and you may learn about another defense strategy: irate alligator lizards defecate freely.

### WOODLANDS, GRASSLANDS, CHAPARRAL

All species of alligator lizard prefer brush, open woodlands, or rocky chaparral, from sea level to 7,000 feet. The only places where you are not likely to find them are deserts and very high elevations. Two of the four species are localized: Madrean (as in

[opposite] Some alligator lizards venture up trees and into shrubs, but most stick to the ground.

the Spanish word, *madre*) is the southeastern Arizona specialty, while California's endemic Panamint alligator lizard, tan with brown stripes, centers its range on the Coso, Inyo, Panamint, and White Mountains. The White Mountains are the ones opposite the Eastern Sierra on the other side of the Owens Valley, so you can look for this species on your next journey to pay tribute to the bristlecone pines.

The other two species occur more broadly. Northern alligator lizard can be found in Washington, Oregon, and Northern California along coastal ranges and in the Sierra Nevada. Southern alligator lizard overlaps with that but continues south into Baja. Tell them apart by the color of the eye: dark in northern, light in southern. Belly scales differ in small ways as well.

Why "alligator" lizards? It's because the large keeled scales on the back and sides of all four species resemble the bony plates found on alligators and crocodiles. The resemblance is due to convergent evolution, not direct relation. The two lineages haven't shared a common ancestor for 280 million years.

**Alligator lizards inhabit a variety of ecosystems, from pine forests to chaparral.**

## HUNGRY, HUNGRIER, HUNGRIEST

Always ready for another trip to the buffet, alligator lizards have scales that contain folds of skin between them. This allows the belly to expand to accommodate large prey . . . or to house the growing eggs, in the case of a pregnant female. Diet consists mostly of insects, spiders, and slugs when juveniles, but larger individuals can feed on other lizards and even small mammals and birds.

Because of their very long bodies, alligator lizards are often confused with snakes.

Can they bite? Of course. How else could they catch their prey? The more important questions is, will they bite *you*? Depends how much you mess around with them. These lizards are not aggressive but will defend themselves from predators and humans. There are several records of alligator lizards effectively deterring snakes by biting them on the head—alligator lizard jaws can snap down and deliver a very decisive nip, and it's not as if the snake can put up its hands to defend itself.

Their main predators include large snakes, birds, and some mammals. Human-caused habitat destruction and fragmentation is another issue, but in many places, alligator lizards seem to adapt, often being found in backyards and culverts. They hide under rocks, logs, and the leaf litter of the forest, but they can also

Crossbands in body and tail can be a good feature to separate them from other lizards.

climb trees, with the aid of their long and somewhat prehensile tail. On average they are shy and secretive, mostly active during early morning or late afternoon, but don't be surprised if you encounter them active during hot nights.

If you do see one, look to see if there's a second one interacting with it. If so, you may be able to add to an ongoing study.

## COMMUNITY SCIENCE SUCCESS STORY

In cool places, mating season occurs in April and May, and the mating couples can stay together for several minutes, even hours. Females in those cool areas lay up to 20 eggs in June and July, but populations in warmer places can breed year around. That's where you come in. As of 2015, scientific literature reported only three dates when southern alligator lizards had been observed mating, but Greg Pauly, herpetologist at the Natural History Museum of Los Angeles County, knew more observations were possible "by crowdsourcing the study of this rarely documented behavior." A call was put out, and everyday nature folks used smart phones to document alligator lizards *in flagrante delicto*. The results surprised even the most optimistic museum staff.

Greg Pauly again: "We have now accumulated 255 observations of mating southern alligator lizards, and 37 observations of northern alligator lizards. We are pretty sure that through community science, we have generated the largest dataset ever on lizard mating."

It sounds cliché, yet it's important and true: the more we look, the more we see.

# desert iguana

## *Dipsosaurus dorsalis*

**FUN FACT**

*Dipsosaurus* derives from the Latin for "thirsty lizard."

| SIZE | FOOD | SPECIES IN OUR AREA |
| --- | --- | --- |
| 4–5.5 inches, plus a tail often longer than body | desert flowers, leaves, arthropods | 1 |

After the Gila monster and chuckwalla, desert iguanas are the third-largest species of lizard in the western United States. The desert iguana has a relatively short, blunt snout, large nostrils, and eyes with yellow irises. The overall coloration serves as camouflage and consists of a light brown reticulated pattern and white spots. Tails are thin and long (usually extending 1.5 times the length of the body) with thin brown bands. Underparts are mostly whitish, with adults having two rust-colored patches on the belly. The sides become a little pinkish, usually early in spring; in many lizards, this is a breeding-season message from

Desert iguanas have relatively short and blunt heads, with pale eyes.

Even the most heat-tolerant species of lizard must find cover away from the desert sun.

Creosote bush–dominated areas like this constitute prime habitat for desert iguanas.

females to males that essentially says, "Knock it off, I've already mated this year!" Females will deposit up to 10 eggs twice per season. Eggs usually hatch in September. Temperatures required for incubation range from a toasty 82°F to a scorching 100°F.

You can find desert iguanas in low- to medium-elevation desert areas (up to ~3,000 feet) in southeastern California, southern Nevada and Utah, and western Arizona. They live in close association with creosote plants and prefer relatively flat, sandy or soft soils.

## HOT TO TROT

Desert iguanas are known to handle the hottest daytime temperatures, surpassing the usual upper heat tolerance (104°F) of all other lizard species. But even they have a limit (115°F), and when the desert is just too hot, they will retreat underground into burrows excavated by them or by kit foxes, desert tortoises, or other lizards. Most of their burrows are located at the base of vegetation, commonly creosote bushes, and they will hibernate during the coldest months.

An adult desert iguana's diet consists mostly of plant material; it is easy to find them foraging on creosote and cacti flowers during blooming season, but they will also feed on leaves and arthropods. Young individuals depend more heavily on arthropods. Both juveniles and adults will eat the feces of other desert iguanas, which helps with digestion of the tough plant cellulose by exchanging gut microbes. Despite their large size, various raptors, foxes, sidewinders, and coachwhip snakes are known to predate them.

## MARKING YOUR HOME

With the help of large pores inside the thighs called femoral pores, desert iguanas produce chemicals that are visible under UV light. Little is known about these chemicals or the sensorial capacity of the species, but the chemicals may be important to mark territories. Like many other species of lizards, they also communicate by doing pushups.

The best way to find this species is to visit the creosote bush flatlands in the Mojave and lower Colorado deserts during spring and summer. Look for them climbing and foraging on the top of the bushes and walk up slowly, watching out for resting animals at the base of the bushes. Driving slowly through these areas can also reward you with some individuals that will shoot across the road right in front of you.

Desert iguanas are among largest lizard species in the western United States.

# chuckwalla

*Sauromalus ater*

**FUN FACT**

*Sauromalus* means “flat lizard,” a reference to their ability to wedge themselves into tight spaces between rocks.

| SIZE | FOOD | SPECIES IN OUR AREA |
|---|---|---|
| up to 9 inches, plus a tail of 6 inches | flowers, buds, fruit, leaves, insects, spiders | 1 |

Chuckwallas are a recognizable part of the folklore and culture of the Mojave and Sonoran deserts in western Arizona, southern Utah and Nevada, and eastern California. After the Gila monster, they are the largest species of lizard native to the continental United States. Another five species in the same genus exist in Baja. They are difficult to mistake: stocky lizards with thick muscular limbs and blunt tails. Coloration is usually dark or black with black bands on the body and tail; bands are present most often in young individuals and females. There is some color variation across the range, including reddish or orange in the backs and tails of males in some populations. With up to 2 pounds of mass, these are *big*; the only other lizards that approach that size in our area would be the Gila monster and the related desert iguana. Desert iguanas are much lighter in color and slimmer overall, with longer, thinner tails.

[opposite] Chuckwallas usually bask and feed close to the safety of their preferred rock crevice.

[below] Hot and low-elevation areas with abundant rocky outcrops like this lava flow are preferred by chuckwallas.

## LIVING THE EXTREMES

Diurnal and well adapted to desert conditions, chuckwallas can remain active even during the hottest parts of the day. However, during the cold months, chuckwallas sometimes hibernate. The diet consists of plants, and they forage in close proximity to the rocky outcrops where they bask and hide. Creosote flowers are a known delicacy for chuckwallas. Just like fence lizards, chuckwallas will also do pushups to signal to invaders and other males when competing for territory; however, they lack the belly patches of fence lizards. Males also use pheromones released by pores in their thighs to mark territories.

## BE CAREFUL, LIVE LONGER

Chuckwallas will usually hide quickly when approached, and often you can hear their thick rough skin rubbing against a rock before you spot their tails disappearing into a crevice. One of the most famous behaviors of the chuckwalla is the way they wedge themselves inside crevices. Once there, they inflate their lungs, to avoid being pulled out by predators. Use a mirror or a bright flashlight to shine some light inside the crevice, and you will usually find them not too far inside, slowly retreating as you try to get closer to them.

Despite the fact that chuckwallas are not aggressive, they occasionally bite when handled, and because of their large size, bites can be painful. Also, keep in mind their long and strong claws, which they use to traverse rough terrain.

Natural predators of chuckwallas include large mammals, birds of prey, and snakes. In captivity, chuckwallas can live over 25 years; about 15 years is more usual in the wild. Females will lay eggs (five to 16) only during years with decent amounts of rain; such years favor vegetation and other resources needed to feed the mother while she is developing the eggs and the young once they hatch after a 72-day incubation period.

**[opposite, top] Populations across different regions present some color variation. Some have red tails; others have red sides.**

**[opposite, bottom] To find chuckwallas, scan a boulder field with binoculars.**

# collared lizards

*Crotaphytus* spp.

**FUN FACT**

Collared lizards are known for running short distances using only their hind legs, at speeds up to 16 miles per hour.

| SIZE | FOOD | SPECIES IN OUR AREA |
| --- | --- | --- |
| 2.5–4.5 inches, plus a tail of up to 10 inches | arthropods, other lizards, plants | 4: Great Basin collared lizard (*C. bicinctores*), eastern collared lizard (*C. collaris*), Sonoran collared lizard (*C. nebrius*), Baja collared lizard (*C. vestigium*) |

Across the American Southwest, collared lizards are some of the most recognizable and colorful species of lizards. Baja and Sonoran collared lizards are found mostly in the southern areas. In contrast, species like the Great Basin collared lizard can be found as far north as eastern Washington and western Idaho. The well-named eastern collared lizard (aka mountain boomer) occurs from Arizona all the way east to the Ozark Mountains in Missouri and Arkansas. It is also the state reptile of Oklahoma.

[opposite] Great Basin collared lizards are among the most iconic species of the desert, and all collared lizards exhibit a wonderful arrangement of color.

## ORNAMENTS IN THE DESERT

As the name implies, collared lizards have distinctive "collar" stripes around the neck and bands on most of the rest of the body. Their long tails can be twice body length, but it is common to find individuals with missing tips, since their tails don't grow back. The rest of the body can vary from a turquoise-green to olive and yellow, with black and white reticulated patterns. Bellies are whitish with no color patches. Males are larger than females and have relatively larger heads. Males are highly competitive and can engage in ferocious fights aided by their powerful jaws, so watch out for those jaws when handling them. Egg-carrying females will signal their pregnancy with red spots or bands on their neck and body. Females lay up to a dozen eggs in the summer, but babies don't receive any parental care after that. Most individuals will live four to seven years in the wild.

[left] Sparse, medium-sized rocks in lowland and mid-elevation desert areas are preferred.

[opposite, top] Tails can easily be twice as long as the rest of the body in length, but many individuals have short tails, which reveal a "lucky break" when something tried to eat them.

[opposite, bottom] Pregnant females like this eastern collared lizard will present red accents to signal males not to bother them.

## CAN'T BE TOO PICKY

Their diet consists mainly of arthropods, but like many other larger lizards, they will prey on small vertebrates if possible, including other lizards and smaller individuals of their own species. Occasionally, collared lizards will also feed on plant matter, including flowers of many desert plant species. Foraging areas are located close to their favorite basking rocks, into which most individuals will quickly retreat when approached. Among the most famous predators of collared lizards are roadrunners, but other birds, snakes, and larger mammals will also hunt them.

When looking for them, use your binoculars to scout for silhouettes on the rocks ahead of you, not only on the top but also the side, where they "hang." In highly visited areas like Navajo Bridge in the Grand Canyon and California's Fossil Falls, individuals will be more tolerant of human presence, and most will let you get pretty close.

Rocky slopes near canyons with medium-sized boulders and abundant low vegetation and old lava flows are good places to look for them. Driving slowly along the road will allow you to get relatively close; watch for sleepy individuals basking on the rocks near the road.

# leopard lizards

## *Gambelia* spp.

**FUN FACT**

Gambel's oak, a common tree in the Southwest, echoes the honoree of the genus name.

| SIZE | FOOD | SPECIES IN OUR AREA |
| --- | --- | --- |
| 3–6 inches; with tail, up to 13 inches | insects, other arthropods, other lizards | 3: Cope's leopard lizard (*G. copeii*), blunt-nosed leopard lizard (*G. sila*), long-nosed leopard lizard (*G. wislizenii*) |

Leopard lizards are medium-sized species and such close relatives of collared lizards that they once were considered the same genus. There are only three species of leopard lizards in the world; all are in the genus *Gambelia*, and all occur in the western United States. The long-nosed leopard lizard is the most widely distributed, inhabiting most of the western arid regions as far north as the interior of Oregon and Idaho, most of Nevada, Utah, western Colorado, Arizona, and most of southern New Mexico. The blunt-nosed leopard lizard is an endemic of the San Joaquin Valley in California; Cope's leopard lizard occurs only in Baja and a tiny area in Southern California. Leopard lizards are found in desert shrub, grassland, creosote plains, and bunchgrass areas from near sea level up to about 6,000 feet.

[opposite, top] As with so many lizards, basking time is the best chance to find leopard lizards. Look for medium-sized rocks along the sides of dirt roads.

[opposite, bottom] The distinctive patchy pattern is what gives leopard lizards their name; however, they are also great predators, just like leopards in Africa and Asia.

### AN APPROPRIATE NAME

The common name comes from a leopard lizard's distinctive dark spotty/patchy color pattern, which covers both body and tail. These patches are less distinctive in Cope's leopard lizard. However, well-marked light-colored crossbars are also present in

many individuals. A pregnant female leopard lizard displays bright red and orange on her sides, neck, and head to tell males to back off. Blunt-nosed leopard lizard females and males are very similar and relatively difficult to tell apart by just looking. Females will lay up to a dozen eggs per year in usually one or two clutches in spring or summer. The number of clutches depends on environmental conditions, such as temperature, rain, and food availability.

Leopard lizards can be found basking on relatively small rocks or even just on open ground.

Leopard lizards are agile jumpers and fast runners. They are famous for being able to run on their hindlimbs for short distances, similar to collared lizards. Just like the mammals of the same name, all leopard lizards are predators and start their hunting activity relatively early in the morning, hiding in cooler places during the hottest parts of the day. They will use their powerful jaws to prey on insects and other arthropods and other lizards, including smaller members of their own species. They can often be found basking on top of small and medium-sized rocks; however, they will also happily bask directly on the ground, sometimes in the middle of dirt roads.

Lowland and mid-elevation areas with dispersed vegetation and soft soils are good habitat choices when looking for leopard lizards.

### SAD COINCIDENCE

Sadly, just as with leopards in many places around the world, blunt-nosed leopard lizards are also endangered. They used to inhabit most of the Central Valley in California, but land conversion into crops, oil drilling, and grazing land for cattle has greatly reduced their habitat. Today, blunt-nosed leopard lizards occupy only tiny portions of their former range. Carrizo Plains National Monument is a good place to look for them, but remember these are protected under California law—look but do not touch.

The other two species are currently not listed under special concern categories, but habitat destruction and encroaching development are likely problems that could affect them in the future.

# fringe-toed lizards

*Uma* spp.

FUN FACT

Fringed toes allow these lizards to run on top of loose sand.

| SIZE | FOOD | SPECIES IN OUR AREA |
| --- | --- | --- |
| 2.5–5 inches, plus a tail of 4 inches | mostly insects, occasionally plants | 5: Yuman Desert fringe-toed lizard (*U. cowlesi*), Coachella Valley fringe-toed lizard (*U. inornata*), Colorado Desert fringe-toed lizard (*U. notata*), Mojave fringed-toed lizard (*U. scoparia*), Mohawk Dunes fringe-toed lizard (*U. thurmanae*) |

With their small ranges, extreme camouflage, and lightning-fast speed, getting a good look at a fringe-toed lizard is the novice herpetologist's holy grail. These lizards are specially adapted to life on the sand: the special scales on their toes form a "fringe," which increases the surface area of the foot and allows them to gracefully run atop loose, windblown sand dunes. The five species may be found in Southern California, western Arizona, northern Baja, and northwestern Sonora. Species are primarily differentiated by range: they can be distinguished from other sand lizard genera (zebra-tailed lizards; earless lizards) by the presence of one or more black blotches on the side of the belly, countersunk lower jaw, and the trademark toes. Each species of fringe-toed lizard has a pattern that differs subtly from others in the genus.

## DESERT LIFE

Walking across sand dunes in *Uma*'s range, you may take a step on what you think is a patch of bare soil, but a tiny eruption followed by Olympic-speed bipedal skittering will indicate that, in fact, you have just stepped on a buried fringe-toed lizard. Their small, granular scales aid in rapid burial in the sand, where they seek refuge from both predators and extreme temperatures. Fringe-toed lizards are known to use rodent burrows as well, but they need to be careful, as these are frequented by another reptile, the sidewinder, which preys on lizards.

While the toes of these lizards may be unique enough to warrant a shout-out in their name, the lizards also have interesting adaptations on their heads. Look closely—does this lizard have a stiff upper lip? No, they're not trying to hide their emotions; the lower jaw is countersunk to prevent sand from getting in their mouths. They also have specially adapted eyelids and ear coverings, also to protect from sand.

[opposite] Mojave fringe-toed lizard pauses for a moment, allowing us to get a good look at one of the dark side blotches on its belly.

Fringe-toed lizards will eat a variety of desert insects, including grasshoppers, beetles, moths, caterpillars, and ants. They have also been recorded eating plants.

Fringe-toed lizards can bury themselves in the sand rapidly to avoid high temps and predators.

## HABITAT AND VIEWING TIPS

Because of their specialized lifestyle on sand dunes, which tend to be isolated between other habitat types, populations of these lizards are also isolated. In May 2020 a new species was described, *Uma thurmanae*, named after actress Uma Thurman for her advocacy of conservation. The species is endemic to the Mohawk Dunes in southwestern Arizona.

Good viewing locations include Kelso Dunes, Mojave National Preserve (Mojave fringe-toed lizard), Algodones Dunes, California (Colorado Desert fringe-toed lizard), and dunes near Yuma, Arizona (Yuman Desert fringe-toed lizard).

Binoculars or a camera are suggested for viewing: because these lizards are so fast, large distances may be required to see one at rest. The best times for viewing are early morning in the spring, before ground temperatures get too hot.

**Fringe-toed lizards are specialized for life in the sand, such as the Kelso Dunes in the Mojave National Preserve.**

# earless lizards and zebra-tailed lizard

## *Callisaurus*, *Cophosaurus*, and *Holbrookia* spp.

**FUN FACT**

These are some of our fastest lizards.

| SIZE | FOOD | SPECIES IN OUR AREA |
| --- | --- | --- |
| 2–4 inches, plus a tail of equal length | insects | 4: zebra-tailed lizard (*Callisaurus draconoides*), greater earless lizard (*Cophosaurus texanus*), elegant earless lizard (*H. elegans*), lesser earless lizard (*H. maculata*) |

Though these sand lizards appear similar at first glance, they are actually quite different and easy to identify by a few basic characteristics. The zebra-tailed lizard is recognized by the tail, which has black rings, giving it the namesake zebra-like appearance. The tail is also often curled up as the animal skitters away, so that the lizard looks like Aladdin's lamp. For the other species, to tell them apart, look for two dark bars on their sides—just in front of the hind legs on *Cophosaurus*, and just behind the front legs on *Callisaurus*. The function of the brightly colored tail is not fully understood but may serve as a signal to predators—"Hey, I see you, and don't bother trying to catch me—I'm way too fast."

Earless lizards come in three choices: greater, lesser, and elegant. The lesser earless lizard has a blunt tail shorter than its body length, distinguishing it from other sand lizards. The other two earless lizards are distinguished by range: in southern Arizona,

A zebra-tailed lizard shows off its namesake trait, the "zebra tail," which it curls up as it runs away from predators.

the elegant earless lizard is present—anywhere else, the greater and lesser earless lizards fill out the map.

### DESERTS-R-US

The zebra-tailed lizard and earless lizards are considered sand lizards, adapted to life in sandy areas. You can find zebra-tailed lizards in the Great Basin, Mojave, and Sonoran deserts; this species may be a good viewing target for a novice herpetologist, because they are more heat-tolerant than other lizards and remain active during midday. Good luck trying to catch one, though—this is one of our fastest lizards!

Greater earless lizards occupy the Chihuahuan Desert and parts of the Sonoran and Mojave deserts. They are active morning and dusk, avoiding the heat of the day. At night they will tuck themselves in by burrowing completely under the sand.

Sand lizards are well adapted for high temperatures and can be seen basking even during the hottest parts of the day.

## FANS OF BUG-TOWN BUFFET

None of the sand lizards are picky eaters: they will sit and wait for insects to walk by and then snatch them. Favorite foods include beetles, caterpillars, ants, wasps—basically your average lunch menu in this habitat and if you are a predator of this size. The lesser earless lizard will occasionally eat smaller lizards, as well. And what eats them? Roadrunners and kestrels and everything else, though being very pale and very fast are always good strategies.

[above left] This is the most common view one gets when trying to chase a zebra-tailed lizard.

[above right] What this lizard lacks in ears, it makes up for in exquisite ventral coloration.

# horned lizards

*Phrynosoma* spp.

**FUN FACT**

Many species shoot blood from their eyes when threatened.

| SIZE | FOOD | SPECIES IN OUR AREA |
|---|---|---|
| 2–4 inches, plus a short tail | insects, preferably ants | 8: Blainville's horned lizard (*P. blainvillii*), Texas horned lizard (*P. cornutum*), pygmy short-horned lizard (*P. douglasii*), greater short-horned lizard (*P. hernandesi*), flat-tailed horned lizard (*P. mcallii*), round-tailed lizard (*P. modestum*), desert horned lizard (*P. platyrhinos*), regal horned lizard (*P. solare*) |

Horned lizards are some of our most charismatic reptiles. They are also known as horny toads, but these animals are not toads at all: this alternative common name comes from a loose translation of the genus name *Phrynosoma* ("toad-bodied"). With 17 species total and eight occurring in the American West, there are many opportunities for a curious herper to see one of these iconic animals. Horned lizards are easily distinguished from other lizard groups by their extremely flattened body (like a pancake), sharp spines ("horns"), and relatively short tails. Within the genus, species are identified by body patterns and the number and arrangement of the horns on the head. These are medium-sized lizards, with bodies averaging a few inches long, though they look bigger, thanks to their sand-dollar bodies and fierce crown of spikes.

Each species has a unique arrangement of "horns"—this is the Texas horned lizard, the largest of the bunch.

This greater short-horned lizard found a nice rock for basking.

To avoid being picked up, horned lizards may duck their heads and elevate their horns.

The smallest of the bunch, the pygmy short-horned lizard, can be seen in the Pacific Northwest; the Texas horned lizard is the largest (of course), though it has a wide range and can be found as far west as Arizona.

## UNIQUE DEFENSE MECHANISMS

The wide, flat bodies of horned lizards, though stylish, do not lend themselves to fast running. Horned lizards instead use camouflage to avoid predators—their cryptic body patterns and sharp protuberances mimic the gravelly soil and dry vegetation of their native habitats. Most species are ground-dwellers that live in deserts or open plains. When located, horned lizards will often stay very still: "You can't see me!" But when crypsis fails, some, but not all, species of horned lizards have another trick up their (short) sleeves: they squirt blood from their eyes (really, a sinus located behind each eye), to confuse and repel predators.

Scientific research has shown that horned lizards respond differently based on the type of predator encountered. Horned lizards can't outrun fast-moving and actively foraging snakes,

Take our word for it, these horns are sharp.

so instead they rely on camouflage and staying still. In contrast, rattlesnakes are ambush or sit-and-wait predators that horned lizards *can*, and do, outrun. The blood squirting has a repellent effect on mammalian predators, like foxes and coyotes.

## DEW-LICKING MYRMECOPHAGES

Ants—and especially harvester ants—are a special delicacy to many horned lizards. Yet as many herpers and naturalists know well, many ants (including harvesters) can have a painful sting. Some species of horned lizards have a special blood factor that detoxifies ant venoms, making them resistant to such stings and allowing them to enjoy the ants for a tasty meal. Each ant has a low nutrient density, so these lizards must eat them in huge quantities (up to 200 ants a day), hence their large stomachs.

Living in arid conditions requires special ways to obtain water. Horned lizards are known to lick dew off of vegetation, and during the rains, they will position their bodies to collect rainwater in their mouths.

# side-blotched lizard

*Uta stansburiana*

**FUN FACT**

Males have different mating strategies based on throat color.

| SIZE | FOOD | SPECIES IN OUR AREA |
|---|---|---|
| 1.5–2.5 inches, plus a tail of equal length | insects | 1 |

One of the most remarkable things about this small lizard is its enormous range and ability to flourish in a variety of environments. Generally, it inhabits arid and semi-arid environments from Washington State to the tip of Baja, and from California to Texas. The side-blotched lizard is one of the most commonly observed lizards in its range, often reaching very high population densities. Because of their small size, these lizards warm up quickly and can be seen in the early morning and late afternoon basking on rocks or the ground. Grasshoppers, ants, beetles, and other arthropods make up their diet. Presence of external ears distinguishes this lizard from earless lizards (*Holbrookia*), and smoother scales distinguishes it from spiny lizards (*Sceloporus*).

**Male side-blotched lizards have different throat colors that correspond with their mating strategies.**

**ROCK, PAPER, SCISSORS**

Overall color is brownish gray, with mottling on the back that can occur in a variety of colors: males often have blue or yellow spotting. The common name is a reference to the dark, well-defined blotch on the side behind the forearms. Male side-blotched lizards come in three flavors based on throat color: blue, orange, and yellow. Thorough study has revealed the complex dynamics that maintain these different color morphs within each population. Throat color is not simply an ornament in these lizards but defines the way that males attract mates:

Males will puff up their throat and do push-ups to defend territory.

- Blue-throated lizards are "monogamous" and guard their mates.

- Orange-throated lizards are the largest and most aggressive. They defend territories with multiple females and mate with multiple females across the season.

- Yellow-throated males mimic females and attempt to sneak matings with their blue and orange counterparts' females.

Because blue-throated males pay close attention to their mates, they are not fooled by the yellows. Blue males will help one another, too—if a yellow is seen trying to sneak in, the blue males will warn one another of the intruder. But orange males, which are larger and more aggressive, can chase off the blues. Orange males are not invincible, though: yellow males, mimicking females, are able to sneak matings with the females of the orange-throated males.

This dynamic results in a rock-paper-scissors mating strategy, in which each male morph "beats" one other yet is "beaten" by the third. Females prefer to mate with whichever morph is most rare in a given season—say, blue. They then give birth to more blues, and thus the rare morph becomes common. Over a space of two to three years, a new morph becomes rare, and the cycle repeats. The stability of morphs varies geographically—in Utah this rotation is less obvious.

[above left] Side-blotched lizards are common across palm and desert habitats.

[above right] They are often found basking on large rocks.

# western fence lizard

*Sceloporus occidentalis*

**FUN FACT**

This spiny lizard fights Lyme disease.

| SIZE | FOOD | SPECIES IN OUR AREA |
| --- | --- | --- |
| 1–4 inches, plus a tail of equal length | insects | 1 |

This is an abundant and common lizard in California, Nevada, Washington, and parts of central Oregon. Medium-sized, it has a long tail and pointed scales. Overall coloration varies from a grayish brown to a darker brown, often with a vertical pattern of interlocking Vs. While western fence lizards are optimized for crypsis ("not being seen-ness"), their other common name, blue bellies, is a direct reference to the showy bright blue patches on the underside of males. These patches are usually outlined in black and do not connect, leaving a thin patch of gray scales between them.

## PUSHUPS AND POWER PLAYS

The western fence lizard is one of the most familiar herps of the American West. Often found basking on rocks and fenceposts on sunny days, these lizards are charismatic and easy to observe. You may notice one doing pushups and head-bobs. Males do this to flash their blue patches to other males as a warning signal, as

**Adult males and some females have "blue bellies," which is another common name for these lizards.**

well as to attract female lizards. The size of the belly patch and the specific shade of blue have been shown to correlate with male fitness in another *Sceloporus* species, the eastern fence lizard, and that probably is true for this lizard, too.

This species can be distinguished by its single throat patch (patches are divided in other spiny lizards) and the yellow on its hindlimbs. As a general rule of thumb, if you are in northern Washington, southwestern Idaho, California, Nevada, or western Utah and you see a lizard with blue belly patches, it's probably a western fence lizard. Several subspecies occur across this lizard's relatively large range, but they are difficult to distinguish without genetic testing.

This species is highly adaptable and can be found in a variety of habitats, including grasslands, scrublands, chaparral, oak and conifer woodlands, and high-elevation open forests. They are also common in disturbed habitats in both urban and rural areas, and can be seen on rocks, logs, tree stumps, woodpiles, walls, and fence posts. Because this species coexists readily with humans, exists in high densities where it is found, and performs conspicuous behaviors, it is an easy viewing target for a novice herper.

[above] At Yosemite National Park and other higher elevations, western fence lizards tend to be more blue.

[opposite] These lizards don't just hang out on fences; they like trees and rocks, too.

In mild climates, they are active year-round, but males perform their most gregarious displays from March to mid-June.

Western fence lizards often look as if they've just heard a bad joke.

You have the best chance of seeing them on sunny days; these sensible lizards prefer warm temperatures and direct sunlight, but don't like it when it is sweltering hot. When frightened, they may scamper to another perch or under vegetation. In places with heavy human traffic, such as state and national parks, they may be more acclimated to humans and allow you to crouch down and get a good look.

**DISEASE, BE GONE!**

The western fence lizard has a superpower: its blood contains a special protein that kills the bacterium that causes Lyme disease. The interaction goes something like this: a tick with the disease-causing bacterium in its guts bites a fence lizard, the protein in the lizard's blood eliminates the bacterium, and the tick is no longer a vector for disease. This protein is incredibly effective; where these lizards occur, only 5% of ticks contain the harmful bacterium, compared to a prevalence of 50% in other areas.

# spiny lizards

*Sceloporus* spp.

**FUN FACT**

Spiny lizards (aka blue bellies) have bright colors underneath . . . and they're not always blue.

| SIZE | FOOD | SPECIES IN OUR AREA |
|---|---|---|
| 2.5–6 inches, plus a long tail | insects | 13: twin-spotted spiny lizard (*S. bimaculosus*), Clark's spiny lizard (*S. clarkii*), southwestern fence lizard (*S. cowlesi*), sagebrush lizard (*S. graciosus*), Yarrow's spiny lizard (*S. jarrovii*), desert spiny lizard (*S. magister*), granite spiny lizard (*S. orcutti*), crevice spiny lizard (*S. poinsettii*), Slevin's bunchgrass lizard (*S. slevini*), plateau fence lizard (*S. tristichus*), prairie fence lizard (*S. undulatus*), yellow-backed spiny lizard (*S. uniformis*), striped plateau lizard (*S. virgatus*) |

This is a diverse group, with about 100 species across North and Central America. People are often familiar with these charismatic lizards, since they are well adapted to human life and abundant where found. Many spiny lizards have large ranges, such as the western fence lizard (previous entry) and the sagebrush lizard, both of which occur through California, the Pacific Northwest, and into the Great Basin. The southwestern fence lizard, plateau fence lizard, and prairie fence lizard were all previously considered one species, but genetic work showed them as distinct: they can be found across the Great Basin region and into the Rocky Mountains.

Other spiny lizards are extremely specialized. Slevin's bunchgrass lizard prefers meadow habitats with abundant bunchgrasses and is currently isolated to mountaintop populations and a few relict lowland areas. Yarrow's spiny lizard, granite spiny lizard, and crevice spiny lizard prefer rocky slopes; rock-dwellers tend

to have larger bodies and more spiny scales. Other spiny lizards, like the desert spiny lizard and the twin-spotted spiny lizard, like it hot—they can be found basking on large rocks in desert scrub communities.

Many spiny lizards earn their name with keeled scales: each scale has a ridge down the center, giving it a rough or "spiny" appearance (hence the common name). All species in this group have the same general body plan but can vary widely in size and coloration. Compare diminutive Slevin's bunchgrass lizard to the large desert spiny lizard. The color of spiny lizards serves two purposes: from the top, lizards are optimized to be cryptic and hide from potential predators like birds of prey and mammals. But hey . . . "Why is that lizard doing pushups?"

Underneath, many species have bright belly patches that they use to signal to other members of their species: "This is my territory—get out!" or, "Isn't my blue stomach nice, don't I seem like a good mate?" Spiny lizards use pushup displays to selectively show off these belly patches as well as their strength. This method allows them to signal to others while remaining cryptic to

[above] This desert spiny lizard shows off its bright throat and belly coloration.

[opposite, top] This pregnant Slevin's bunchgrass lizard was marked for study by coauthors Erin and José.

[opposite, bottom] The striped plateau lizard is one of a few species that have lost the blue belly patches.

overhead predators. The number and rate of pushups varies between species, too.

Spiny lizards mate in the spring, and both males and females can mate with multiple partners. Most spiny lizards lay eggs in mid to late summer, but some, like Yarrow's spiny lizard, give birth to live young. Clutch size varies from as few as two to as many as 24. All spiny lizards eat insects; larger individuals might eat other young lizards, too. Spiny lizards are active during the day and take shelter under rocks or vegetation at night. Good viewing times are early in the morning and late afternoon during spring and summer. Some species are skittish and will run under rocks or around trees if they see you—binoculars work well to spot them from afar.

Yarrow's spiny lizard lives at high elevations and gives birth to live young.

# night lizards

## *Xantusia* spp.

**FUN FACT**

Night lizards are—wait for it—mostly nocturnal.

| SIZE | FOOD | SPECIES IN OUR AREA |
| --- | --- | --- |
| 1.5–4 inches; with tail, up to 7 inches | insects, other arthropods | 8: Arizona night lizard (*X. arizonae*), Bezy's night lizard (*X. bezyi*), sandstone night lizard (*X. gracilis*), Henshaw's night lizard (*X. henshawi*), island night lizard (*X. riversiana*), Sierra night lizard (*X. sierrae*), desert night lizard (*X. vigilis*), Wiggins' night lizard (*X. wigginsi*) |

Night lizards are usually small, secretive, difficult-to-see species that live under rocks or dense, dead plant material. They inhabit most low- to mid-elevation deserts in California, Nevada, Utah, and Arizona. They are also found in chaparral, coastal sagebrush, yucca forests, and Joshua tree woodlands, from sea level to over 9,000 feet.

At first sight, night lizards resemble small geckos, which are their distant relatives. Their bodies are covered with small round and bumpy scales, with larger flat scales covering the relatively flat head. The head's flattened shape helps them to move into rock crevices. Eyes lack eyelids and, as with snakes, they are covered by transparent scales. Tails are relatively thick and shorter in length than the rest of the body. The largest species in the group is the island night lizard, which occurs exclusively in the Channel Islands. Mainland species are small, rarely reaching 2.5 inches of

[above] Like all night lizards, desert night lizards resemble small geckos.

[below] Enlarged scales cover only the head, while the body has smaller, more granular scales.

body length. Most species have a dark spotted or blotched pattern on the back and plain light-colored bellies.

Yes, night lizards are more active during the night and can occasionally be found crossing trails in rocky areas. During the day they seek refuge from high temperatures by taking cover. Your best chance to find them is by carefully lifting dead vegetation like old yucca stumps, usually near rocky areas. Remember that these microhabitats are very sensitive, and you should replace everything you move. Night lizards are very sensitive to temperature changes, and even human body temperature can be deadly for them.

Night lizards feed on insects and other small arthropods like spiders, scorpions, and centipedes. They have relatively slow life cycles, with individuals taking several years to reach sexual maturity. Most species give birth to live young in small litters of two to four, usually in late summer and early fall.

Desert night lizards spend most of their time in rock crevices or on the ground near vegetation clumps like these Joshua trees.

## WINTER FAMILIES AND RELATIVES ABROAD

Night lizards have social structures, something that is not very common among most reptiles. Young individuals do not venture too far from the yucca or rock hometown where they are born. During the cold months, they will congregate to help maintain a more stable temperature. This is another aspect to keep in mind, so please return any individual to the spot where you find it.

Most night lizards increase their activity at dusk but usually don't move too far from their relatives.

At a larger scale, night lizards belong to a relatively small family of species that occur from the American Southwest to Panama, except for one species in Cuba. Despite the fact that they occur only in dry areas of the United States, their close relatives in Central and South America are found on the damp rainforest floor. Much of the biology of these species is unknown. Many populations are isolated, and the actual diversity of this group is poorly understood.

# skinks

*Plestiodon* spp.

**FUN FACT**

Unlike most reptiles, skinks have scales reinforced by bone.

| SIZE | FOOD | SPECIES IN OUR AREA |
| --- | --- | --- |
| 2.5–5.5 inches, plus a tail often twice as long | insects, other arthropods | 5: mountain skink (*P. callicephalus*), Gilbert's skink (*P. gilberti*), many-lined skink (*P. multivirgatus*), Great Plains skink (*P. obsoletus*), western skink (*P. skiltonianus*) |

Skinks are secretive, small to medium-sized lizards usually found hiding under leaf litter, logs, or rocks. In the western United States, they are found from the Mexican border through most of the western Great Plains and along the Pacific Coast to Canada. This range encompasses a variety of ecosystems, including deserts, pine forests, oak and deciduous forests, grasslands, and mountainous rocky areas, from sea level to almost 9,000 feet.

Several characteristics make skinks difficult to mistake for any of our other lizards. One of the most evident is their smooth shiny skin with semicircular scales reinforced by bone. This smooth skin allows them to pass effortlessly under leaf litter and through grasses, and their short limbs mean that skinks sometimes move in a snake-like fashion, similar to how alligator lizards "slither." The neck is not very evident in their cylindrical bodies; if you're trying to loop one with the herpers' trick of using a string and a fishing pole, this makes them almost impossible to catch. Juveniles of many species have bright blue or red tails that fade to brown with age. Most species have some type of lines or patterns along their backs or sides.

When threatened by predators, skinks are able to detach their tails as an escape strategy. However, like many lizards, getting rid of the tail is a last resort. Tails are reservoirs of fat and energy and expensive for the individual to rebuild. Lizards that lose their tails will be less likely to find a mate, reproduce, and survive. Be very careful when handling any lizard, since their wiggly, slippery nature makes them difficult to handle and tails can get damaged easily.

Skinks are predators, feeding mostly on small insects, mollusks, spiders, and other arthropods. Many of these species give birth to live young, but in the United States most lay two to 10 eggs

[above] Longitudinal lines are characteristic in most skinks.

[opposite] Many species have blue tails that fade as the individual gets older.

Skinks are secretive; often, the only way to find them is by checking under logs or other kinds of cover.

at the beginning of the summer. Warm and moist conditions are the best time to go looking for these species, so try flipping—carefully!—logs and rocks. Many skinks bask right on top of their homes in small sunny openings in the forest.

## AUSTRAL RELATIVES

Our skinks belong to the Scincidae, a large family of lizards. With over 1,500 species worldwide, they are present on every continent except Antarctica and come in much more diverse shapes than the ones we find in the Americas.

Unlike the skinks in the United States, which are small and shy, several of their Australian and Indonesian cousins can be very large, diurnal, and dominate the rocks in their environment, just as chuckwallas do here. The largest species of skink in the world is the semi-arboreal Solomon Island skink, which can exceed 32 inches from head to tip of the tail. Other species like the blue-tongued skink are common in the pet trade. A final example of the diversity of this group would be the crocodile skinks, found on some islands in and around Papua New Guinea: those look a lot more like a dragon than they do like a traditional skink.

# whiptail lizards

## *Aspidoscelis* spp.

**FUN FACT**

Some species consist only of clonal females.

| SIZE | FOOD | SPECIES IN OUR AREA |
| --- | --- | --- |
| 2–5.5 inches, plus a tail often twice as long | insects, preferably termites, ants | 17: Arizona striped whiptail (*A. arizonae*), canyon spotted whiptail (*A. burti*), gray checkered whiptail (*A. dixoni*), Chihuahuan spotted whiptail (*A. exsanguis*), Gila spotted whiptail (*A. flagellicauda*), little white whiptail (*A. gypsi*), orange-throated whiptail (*A. hyperythra*), little striped whiptail (*A. inornata*), New Mexico whiptail (*A. neomexicana*), Colorado checkered whiptail (*A. neotesselata*), Pai striped whiptail (*A. pai*), Sonoran spotted whiptail (*A. sonorae*), checkered whiptail (*A. tesselata*), tiger whiptail (*A. tigris*), desert grassland whiptail (*A. uniparens*), plateau striped whiptail (*A. velox*), red-backed whiptail (*A. xanthonota*) |

Listen carefully: do you hear rustling in the leaf litter, or disturbances in the sand? It might be an actively foraging whiptail lizard, which rarely stays still and has characteristically nervous, twitchy movements. Whiptail lizards are capable of running extremely fast for short distances and are known to dart between patches of vegetation or large rocks; catching one is no easy task.

Whiptails have a distinctive body plan, one that differs from other lizards in the West—slightly elongated, thin bodies, pointy snouts, and extremely long tails that are often twice as long as the body. Many have stripes on the back; others are spotted. Many

A Sonoran spotted whiptail hangs out in the Chiricahua Mountains of Arizona.

It gets hot in the desert, and whiptails have to take water where they can find it, even from a leaky hose.

have a bluish wash; others are brown to rust in color. The small, granular scales are difficult to count but are an important feature in distinguishing one whiptail species from another. In our area, whiptails can be found from desert scrub to grasslands to forests, and everywhere in between. Color is a highly variable feature between sex- and age-classes within species, making proper identification difficult even for seasoned herpetologists.

## NO MALES REQUIRED

Perhaps one of the most interesting aspects of whiptail biology is the repeated evolution of all-female lineages. In an all-female (unisexual) species, the entire species consists only of female individuals, which lay eggs (unfertilized) that are basically clones of their mother. How do such species evolve? Usually, unisexual lineages are the product of hybridization, either between two distinct species, or between a unisexual species and one of its parental species. The latter case is known as a backcross.

The evolution of unisexuality is thought to be advantageous for colonizing new areas: by eliminating the need for males, a single

female individual can enter an area, lay eggs, and effectively start a new population on her own. There are also disadvantages, including loss of genetic diversity.

Individuals in all-female lineages may still engage in mating behaviors and what is known as pseudo-copulation, in which females mimic the copulatory behaviors of male-female species. In some species, this behavior promotes egg-laying in individuals compared to those who do not perform the behavior.

[above] A tiger whiptail tries to hide from the camera.

[below] A female checkered whiptail. How do we know? The whole species is made of females.

# threadsnakes

*Rena* spp.

FUN FACT

Oldest snake lineage in our area.

| SIZE | FOOD | SPECIES IN OUR AREA |
| --- | --- | --- |
| up to 15 inches | ants, termites, other arthropods | 2: New Mexico threadsnake (*R. dissecta*), western threadsnake (*R. humilis*) |

Threadsnakes are often mistaken for worms, but look closely and you will see the overlapping scales.

At first glance, it can be hard to believe that threadsnakes are, in fact, snakes. They seem like a three-way cross between an earthworm, a millipede, and something odd, like maybe a legless lizard. But make no mistake, these tiny, unassuming creatures are snakes, and very cool ones at that. The larger group that these snakes belong to diverged from all the other snakes in our area about 120 million years ago. In other words, this is a very old lineage, and one of the very oldest snake groups on Earth. Don't think this snake is primitive, though: the persistence of threadsnakes for all these years is a testament to how well adapted they are.

The western threadsnake lives in desert and scrub habitats in the southern parts of California, Arizona, and New Mexico, into southwestern Texas. The New Mexico threadsnake is found only in that state and southeastern Arizona. The two species are nearly impossible to distinguish on looks alone, and ecologically they are quite similar. Here we will discuss their generalities.

Found in the early evenings and through the night, these nocturnal snakes spend much of their time burrowed in the sand or hiding under cover objects. Hiding is one of this snake's main defenses against predators, although they may also wriggle and writhe and exude a stinky musk that is quite potent despite their small size. Another reason to burrow into the sand? Looking for ants and their relatives to snack on. Threadsnakes hibernate during the winter and emerge in spring to mate. They lay up to eight eggs underground in late summer.

**Finding a threadsnake is all about being in the right place at the right time.**

Threadsnakes are usually light pink in color with a shiny finish. Their eyes are significantly reduced and hide under semi-translucent scales, and their tails contain a spine at the very tip which they may attempt to poke you with during handling. It won't hurt though. This snake is extremely thin; it will probably slip between your fingers before you even notice it is gone.

Threadsnakes are great burrowers and can disappear into the sand or rocks as soon as they are spotted.

To find a threadsnake, you will need persistence and luck. Try flipping rocks and cover objects in the early evening or walking along dirt roads at night with a headlamp. Many novice herpers may be surprised to learn that this is a long-awaited "lifer" for more experienced naturalists. As the expression goes, it may be small, but it very much is worth the wait.

# boas

## *Charina* and *Lichanura* spp.

**FUN FACT**

Related to the tropical boa constrictors, which can grow over 10 feet long.

| SIZE | FOOD | SPECIES IN OUR AREA |
|---|---|---|
| 2–3 feet | mostly small mammals, occasionally lizards, other snakes, birds | 4: rubber boa (*C. bottae*), southern rubber boa (*C. umbratica*), California rosy boa (*L. orcutti*), rosy boa (*L. trivirgata*) |

This rosy boa is gray, but the species is highly variable.

The boas are fairly thick-bodied snakes whose heads do not get much bigger around than their necks or the rest of their bodies. Rubber boas occupy the north of our region; southern rubber boas are just in the mountains of Southern California, and the variable rosy boa may be several species, but if so, they collectively go from Southern California, down Baja, and across Arizona and into northern Mexico. If you are a splitter, the rosy boa species divide into two in southern Arizona.

The rubber boa is basically gray and feels rubbery. Rosy boa is gray with brown stripes.

Another very typical color pattern for a rosy boa. Note how the head is almost same size as the neck.

## FRIENDLY SNAKES (UNLESS YOU'RE A GOPHER)

Most snakes will bite if provoked, but on average, these snakes (the rosy boa in particular) have docile personalities and will usually let you handle them. They do well in captivity, and many color morphs have been developed. If herpetology needed a goodwill ambassador, the rosy boa would make a good choice.

In the wild, boas forage in loose soil and bark, dense shade, rocky ravines and cliffs, and around old logs. They can be found from sea level to 10,000 feet and are fairly tolerant of cool weather. If they have located a perfect lunch item—let's say it is the desert woodrat (*Neotoma lepida*)—the head strikes with a lightning-fast jab, the sharp teeth keep the target from escaping, and then the coils of the body wrap up the prey and cinch tight, like a rope tying off a sack. One might think this is death by crushing, but the actual mechanism of death can vary; usually, it consists of interrupting blood flow, thus stopping the heart.

What if a boa has found a nest with several nestlings? The coils can constrict multiple items at once. Proof of that comes from an observation by a herpetologist, who caught a rubber boa for photography. The snake did not like being handled and regurgitated lunch: not one, not two, but three recently ingested western moles. In a morbid coincidence, the rubber boa's specific epithet, *bottae*,

Our boas are related to the famous boa constrictors of South America, like this northern boa on a branch in Mexico.

honors 19th-century naturalist Paul-Émile Botta. He has a common gopher named after him too, Botta's pocket gopher (*Thomomys bottae*). Patronymic cannibalism: if a rubber boa catches a gopher, one *bottae* will eat the other, and we bet it won't feel any remorse.

## HIDE 'N' SEEK

If threatened, the rosy boa coils up, plays dead, and sticks its tail out as a last-ditch effort to direct the predator's attention to the tail, not the head. Chemical weapons form defensive barrier number two, since it can release a noxious stench from anal glands. Odds are, you won't experience this personally (if you do, you're doing something wrong), and as one biologist once put it, "They're as calm and easy to get along with as you are. If you're mean and riled up, they will be too." This is probably true about most interactions in life.

# western diamondback rattlesnake

*Crotalus atrox*

**FUN FACT**

Fossils for this species go back 3 million years.

| SIZE | FOOD | SPECIES IN OUR AREA |
| --- | --- | --- |
| 1–6 feet | rats, mice, lizards, birds | 1 |

This common, thick-bodied snake is found in California deserts and across Arizona to New Mexico and Texas, as well as in northern Mexico. Adult diamondbacks weigh 3–6 pounds and average about 4 feet long (but on occasion pass 6 feet). Of all North American rattlesnakes, only the eastern diamondback grows larger.

## DIAMONDS ARE A SNAKE'S BEST FRIEND

Common names for this species range from buzz snake to Texas rattler and checker-back. Body color varies but most often is brown, beige, gray, or pink, over which darker squares, diamonds, bars, or blotches pattern evenly down to a black-and-white striped tail. Those diamonds often are outlined with a dark border, which is itself outlined by a pale line, making a very attractive pattern—and also breaking up the silhouette, so you can walk right past one in a pile of sticks and leaves and never notice. The face shows a broad, dark stripe running diagonal down the cheek, sort of like a bandit mask crossed with a racing stripe.

[opposite, top] Often you will find coiled individuals near their burrows, waiting for the night to come.

[opposite, bottom] Western diamondbacks occur in many color phases, from gray and brown to reddish and pink.

## COMBAT DANCING AND MARACA TAILS

This is a lowland and foothill species, occurring in brushy deserts, grasslands, forests, and on rocky slopes up to 8,000 feet. In Arizona it is also seen on (or near) golf courses. It is most active March through October, at dawn and dusk and in evenings, especially in high summer. In most habitats it spends the coolest months in quasi-hibernation, slowing down metabolism and waiting for warmer days and denser populations of mice, squirrels, rabbits, and gophers. (They also eat lizards, frogs, and birds.) In spring, males assert dominance by combat dancing, with each one reared up head-high and trying to pin the other, like two wrestlers with their hands tied behind their backs.

These rattlesnakes have rhomboid patches on their backs (hence, diamondback).

Female diamondbacks are viviparous, which means that the mama keeps fertilized eggs inside her body and gives birth to live young. One herpetologist who shall remain unnamed had caught an viviparous snake species in the wild and needed to bring it home to the lab. He secured it in a box inside his carry-on bag, with air for it to breathe. He didn't know it was pregnant until he noticed baby snakes crawling down the aisle. They had wiggled out of the air holes. "Snakes on a plane" indeed—luckily it was a red-eye flight, and everybody around him was asleep. He rounded up the babies and stowed them in a smaller, tighter box.

The genus name comes from the Latin for "castanets," and all adult rattlesnakes can rattle, shaking a row of dried segments at the end of the tail. As you approach, it may coil and not make any sound at all, waiting silently until you pass. If it does start to rattle, it is a raspy, hissy, buzzing sound, audible 20 feet or more away—if you've not heard it before, check online before hiking in rattlesnake country.

The rattle itself might have 10 or more segments. (If the snake is a baby, it has just one initial segment, called the button.) Contrary to popular myth, the number of segments indicates health more than direct age; new segments are added with each shedding event, when the snake emerges from the old skin with a shiny new coat. A healthy rattlesnake might shed up to three times a year, but over time, some segments will break off, so a 20-year-old snake could have a rattle only as long as one on a snake half its age.

Diamondbacks can usually be distinguished from other rattlesnakes in our area by the equally sized black and white rings on their tails.

## STAYIN' ALIVE

Hawks and eagles and foxes and bobcats all want to eat snakes, this one included. Other participants in the landscape vary in their responses. A horse may react with fear, curiosity, or indifference, depending on the circumstances and how its rider, if present, reacts. (Horses can't breathe through their mouths, so a horse bitten by a rattlesnake on the nose may suffocate from the swelling, and not be killed by the venom directly.) Squirrels and kangaroo rats know a foe when they meet one; they will sound alarm calls, dance and bluff charge, kick sand, and in general create a ruckus in defense of themselves and their clan. Birds, too, will fuss and scold, mobbing any snake out in daytime.

Finally, a cautionary note about toxins. Since the diamondback makes its living eating small and midsized mammals, it comes equipped with both venom and fangs, neither of which you want to interact with. The bite can be lethal, so unless you speak Parseltongue, stay safe by remembering the twin rules of *distance* and *respect*.

# sidewinder

## *Crotalus cerastes*

**FUN FACT**

From baseball teams to air-to-air missiles, the uses of the word *sidewinder* in pop culture are legion.

| SIZE | FOOD | SPECIES IN OUR AREA |
|---|---|---|
| 1–2.5 feet | rodents, lizards, birds | 1 |

Sidewinders are an iconic species of the American Southwest, and as rattlesnakes go, are the ones best adapted to pure desert. The S of their sideways curls reduces slipping on steep dunes and also helps prevent too much contact with a superheated surface.

This species is almost always a pale snake: tan, light gray, cream, or pinky beige, with contrasting dark diamonds or splotches along the middle of the back. It's not very large, which makes sense, given the harsh environment—it has to make do with pocket mice more often than woodrats and rabbits. It occurs in the Mojave and Sonoran deserts, from below sea level to 6,000 feet. Expect these snakes in both sandy and rocky areas but almost always around "true" desert plants, like creosote and mesquite. Like other rattlesnakes, sidewinders are ambush predators, mostly nocturnal, and they spend their daytime hours hiding at the base of shrubs, slightly buried or in burrows made by other animals. Like other members of the subfamily Crotalinae, sidewinders do not lay eggs but give birth to two to 18 live young.

[above] Sidewinders leave arguably the only snake track that can be identify with certainty. The hook on the J-shaped track indicates the direction of movement.

[opposite] "Horns" are one of the most distinctive features of sidewinders.

Famous for "swimming" across sand, sidewinders can also climb shrubs and small bushes.

Have we said it enough, about being careful around venomous snakes? This snake is one of the ones with potentially lethal venom. Please don't get bit—we all want you to stick around for the second edition.

## AN INTERESTING SNAKE WITH INTERESTING BEHAVIORS

Check this out: baby sidewinders can stick together and form "balls" for weeks, plugging the entrance of their natal burrow and producing their own heat by rubbing against each other to keep a stable temperature. Mama sidewinders will take care of the young until they shed for the first time. After this, the young start dispersing. Another fact? Young ones use the tip of their tails to simulate worms or caterpillars and attract small lizards. Adult sidewinders prey on kangaroo rats, pocket mice, gophers, and other animals. During the cold months, individuals can remain active during the day and prey on desert iguanas and other lizards. Their relatively slender bodies also allow them to climb small shrubs and hunt birds and nestlings.

## SSSS-SIDEWINDING

Sidewinders receive their name because of their sidewinding locomotion. They are also the only viper in our region with modified scales that look like "horns" above their eyes. Their tracks consist of a parallel row of S- or J-shaped lines; both looks are distinctive and easily recognizable. The "hook" of the J points in the direction of travel.

Sidewinding is used in other regions of the world by species that are completely unrelated to ours. Sand vipers, McMahon's viper, and the Namib sidewinding adder all use these movements to keep their bodies as cool as possible and improve efficiency when moving in loose, sandy areas. Biologists call this convergent evolution; dancers just want to know how the animals make it look so effortless.

# rattlesnakes

## *Crotalus* and *Sistrurus* spp.

**FUN FACT**

Rattlesnakes exist only in the Americas and give birth to live young.

| SIZE | FOOD | SPECIES IN OUR AREA |
| --- | --- | --- |
| 1–4.5 feet | small mammals, reptiles, birds | 12: Arizona black rattlesnake (*C. cerberus*), rock rattlesnake (*C. lepidus*), speckled rattlesnake (*C. mitchellii*), black-tailed rattlesnake (*C. molossus*), northern Pacific rattlesnake (*C. oreganus*), twin-spotted rattlesnake (*C. pricei*), red diamond rattlesnake (*C. ruber*), Mojave rattlesnake (*C. scutulatus*), tiger rattlesnake (*C. tigris*), prairie rattlesnake (*C. viridis*), ridge-nosed rattlesnake (*C. willardi*), massasauga (*S. catenatus*) |

The American Southwest is a diversity hotspot for rattlesnakes, and Arizona has more rattlesnake species than any other state. All but the massasauga are in the genus *Crotalus*. Like all vipers in the United States, rattlesnakes have a heat-sensing pit between the nose and the eyes that allows them to detect their warm-blooded prey. The rattle is composed of interlocking segments

**It is not rare to find individuals with broken or incomplete rattles, like this prairie rattlesnake.**

and is not found on any other species group. A new segment is added every time the individual sheds its skin.

Rattlesnakes occur from sea level to 11,500 feet in a variety of habitats, from forests to rocky outcrops and deserts. Some species, like the ridge-nosed and the twin-spotted rattlesnakes, are found on a few peaks in southeastern Arizona, southwestern New Mexico, and northern Mexico. Others, like the prairie rattlesnake, have large ranges; the prairie rattlesnake occurs from northern Mexico all the way to the Canadian border.

Black-tailed rattlesnakes are found from low elevation deserts to pine-oak forest.

### JUST KEEP YOUR DISTANCE

Rattlesnakes are not evil organisms trying to chase you down and harm you. However, they do have well-evolved tools that they use to procure food and defend themselves. Those include venom, foldable, hypodermic-needle-like fangs, and a lightning-fast strike mode that allows them to hit their targets from a surprising distance.

The northern Pacific rattlesnake, which occurs from Baja to British Columbia, tolerates cooler habitats than other rattlesnakes.

Venom is an energetically costly resource that rattlesnakes need to immobilize and digest their prey. Rattlesnakes will most likely use their famous rattle and hiss to warn you to leave them alone. In some cases, rattlesnakes will deliver "dry bites" in which little to no venom is injected. The chemical composition of snake venom is variable; it can depend on species, geography, age, or the health of the individual snake. Some species, like the Mojave rattlesnake, are notably more dangerous than others because of higher concentrations of neurotoxins that interrupt the signals from the brain to the body of their prey.

**In contrast to big snakes like western diamondbacks, even a full-grown twin-spotted rattlesnake rarely surpasses 20 inches.**

### NICHE PARTITIONING

Every organism fills a specific role in an ecosystem. These roles can be narrow in specialist species and very wide in generalist species, which normally overlap to some degree with other generalist species. Rattlesnakes are no different, and as a rule of thumb, the more species you find in an area, the smaller their niches are. Rock rattlesnakes are often associated with rocky outcrops in

mountainous areas; prairie rattlesnakes (unsurprisingly) with open areas. Twin-spotted rattlesnakes are limited to rocky slopes in the U.S. Southwest and northern Mexico.

Widespread or rare, rattlesnakes play important ecological roles. One of the main ones is to control rodent and other small mammal populations. They also constitute the food of many other animals, like roadrunners and even kingsnakes. If you hear one, hold still, find out where it is, and back away slowly—but reach for your camera too, since you'll want to remember what may be the best animal sighting of the day.

The prairie rattlesnake presents great variability across its range, its subspecies elevated to species status by some scientists.

# Sonoran coral snake

*Micruroides euryxanthus*

**FUN FACT**
Coral snakes are venomous, in the same family as cobras and sea snakes.

| SIZE | FOOD | SPECIES IN OUR AREA |
|---|---|---|
| 1–1.5 feet | small lizards, other snakes | 1 |

The Sonoran coral snake is one of the smallest species of coral snakes. They are shy and secretive snakes that inhabits mostly rocky areas in upland deserts of southern Arizona and southwestern New Mexico, at elevations of up to 6,000 feet. Their flat heads (with almost no distinguishable neck) and slim bodies help them to live underground, where they catch small lizards, skinks, and small snakes. Unlike all other venomous snakes native to the United States, which give birth to live young, coral snakes lay eggs, two to six per clutch.

[opposite, top] You will most likely encounter the Sonoran coral snake at night, since it usually hides underground during the day.

[opposite, bottom] The coral snake pattern is among the most recognizable pattern of any animal. However, many non-venomous species also copy this design.

## THE SLIM-HEADED FARTING SNAKE

Coral snakes are a diverse group of over 100 species in the Americas (mostly in South America), and there are even a few that don't have brightly colored rings on their bodies. All coral snakes have round pupils and lack the distinctive "triangular" head of vipers. Many species are easily confused with non-venomous species.

When threatened, coral snakes have a variety of defenses. Besides the obvious warning coloration, some coral snakes will

hide their head under their own body, while coiling the tail and moving it to imitate a second "head." This allows them to distract potential predators from their most vital parts. Another strategy is to produce an audible "fart," or cloacal popping.

### "RED ON YELLOW KILLS A FELLOW" (IS A RATHER INACCURATE RHYME)

All coral snakes have potent neurotoxic venom that they inject into their prey using relatively small, fixed fangs. The Sonoran coral snake, like many (but not all) coral snakes, has a very distinctive pattern, with a black head that starts a pattern of yellow (or white) / red / yellow (or white) / black, and so on, until the tail, where only yellow/white and black rings are present.

These warning colors are mimicked by numerous species, including kingsnakes, milk snakes, long-nosed snakes, shovel-nosed snakes, and groundsnakes. The folk rhyme "Red on black,

This long-nosed snake is one of several non-venomous species that copy the coral snake pattern, hoping to fool potential predators.

friend of Jack / Red on yellow kills a fellow" is often taught to help distinguish a coral snake from a mountain kingsnake, but many coral snakes (and some mimics) do not follow this pattern. All that glitters is not gold, and all that is red and black is not dangerous. *If in doubt, don't touch.*

Coral snake bites are relatively rare, mostly because the species are very secretive and because their mouth and fangs are small. Most incidents with humans occur when someone is handling them carelessly. Always avoid handling wild animals and *never* handle a snake without being sure about their species ID and without having the right training and permits. It is safer for you and for the animal, too.

## FAMOUS RELATIVES

In the western United States, the Sonoran coral snake is the only representative of the family Elapidae and is the only one in the genus *Micruroides*, which sets it apart from other coral snakes of the Americas (which are all in the genus *Micrurus*). However, despite the "solo" status here, other elapids are widely distributed around the world. Sea snakes, king cobras, death adders, and even black mambas belong to this family. The yellow-bellied sea snake can wash up on Southern California beaches during warm water years but is rarely found north of the tropics.

# smooth green snake

*Opheodrys vernalis*

FUN FACT

Males are usually shorter than females snout-to-vent, but with longer tails.

| SIZE | FOOD | SPECIES IN OUR AREA |
| --- | --- | --- |
| 10–20 inches | insects, spiders | 1 |

When looking at a photo of this snake, you might think its bright green color would render it easy to spot. But consider where this snake lives—in grassy areas such as meadows, marshes, and forests. That means that its green color makes it very cryptic. Though difficult to locate, this is usually a docile snake when handled. This snake is eaten by birds of prey and mammals such as foxes, raccoons, and bears. The small size, bright coloration, and gentle disposition of this snake make it an attractive pet, but illegal collecting has contributed to significant declines in wild populations. When approached, the smooth green snake will likely flee and may also produce a foul-smelling musk from its cloaca. In warm weather, this snake can be active both day and night.

Smooth green snakes have a range that extends from eastern North America west to Saskatchewan and south to Utah, Colorado, and New Mexico.

In our area, this species can be found in eastern Utah, western Colorado, and the mountains in the center of New Mexico, though its range extends substantially to the northeast. Its closest relative, the rough green snake, is similar in appearance but occurs east of the Continental Divide. Another green snake in our area is the green ratsnake, which is found only in extreme southeastern Arizona; it has slightly rougher scales and is much larger overall.

The smooth green snake feasts on insects, killing them by striking or swallowing whole. The use of insecticides can negatively affect this snake, especially in riparian areas, by removing its main prey items. Despite a seemingly large range, this snake exists in patchy populations: it is affected by a variety of threats, such as grazing, road building, recreation that damages riparian areas, and other types of habitat destruction.

The smooth green snake mates in the spring, and females lay one or two clutches of eggs in mid to late summer. Some populations in northern areas have been seen nesting communally; they may also hibernate communally during the winter.

**Generally hidden under logs, rocks, or vegetation, smooth green snakes are difficult to find.**

# patch-nosed snakes

*Salvadora* spp.

**FUN FACT**

They can inflate their bodies when threatened.

| SIZE | FOOD | SPECIES IN OUR AREA |
| --- | --- | --- |
| 1.5–3 feet | lizards, small mammals, other snakes, reptile eggs, bird eggs | 2: mountain patch-nosed snake (*S. grahamiae*), western patch-nosed snake (*S. hexalepis*) |

A western patch-nosed snake from the Mojave National Preserve stays still for a brief moment.

Patch-nosed snakes follow the same basic body plan as our racers—long, thin body and large eyes—with the exception of a large, flat scale on the nose that appears almost like a shield. Active during the day, these snakes use their incredible speed to hunt small mammals and reptiles and their eggs. Though not venomous to humans, these snakes do possess enlarged teeth at the back of their mouth ("rear fangs"), which may be used to envenomate prey. If you are lucky enough to spot one, it will likely just dart away; if aggravated, it might puff up its body and strike at you.

The western patch-nosed snake is found broadly across the Southwest (California, Nevada, Arizona, and New Mexico) from sea level to 7,000 feet. It prefers open areas such as grasslands,

plains, and desert scrub, where it moves quickly across sandy and rocky substrates. Overall color is gray to light green with two prominent, dark stripes along the sides of the body, which are often not solid but mottled. The mountain patch-nosed snake is similar in appearance, but body stripes are more solid. This species prefers rocky habitats within woodlands; it occurs in southeastern Arizona and across New Mexico and Texas. Patch-nosed snakes are thought to be common where they occur, but sightings are rare—the combination of cryptic coloration, speed, and an affinity for burrowing makes them difficult to spot. Mostly terrestrial, they will occasionally climb vegetation. Patch-nosed snakes mate in spring and lay three to 12 eggs in mid-summer; the hatchlings appear in late summer.

**One theory behind the "patch nose" is that it is used to help the snake dig into loose soil and locate reptile eggs.**

# racers and whipsnakes

*Coluber* and *Masticophis* spp.

**FUN FACT**

These are some of our fastest snakes.

| SIZE | FOOD | SPECIES IN OUR AREA |
| --- | --- | --- |
| up to 75 inches | small vertebrates | 6: common racer (*C. constrictor*), Sonoran whipsnake (*M. bilineatus*), coachwhip (*M. flagellum*), Baja California coachwhip (*M. fuliginosus*), California whipsnake (*M. lateralis*), striped whipsnake (*M. taeniatus*) |

Racers is a generic term used to describe several groups of snakes across the globe; in our area, it refers mainly to snakes in the genera *Coluber* and *Masticophis*. Both common names, racers and whipsnakes, refer to the fast nature and long, slim bodies of these snakes. Unlike many snakes in our area, racers

Striped whipsnakes are some of our fastest snakes.

and whipsnakes tend to be active during the day; notice how large their eyes are compared to other snakes. They often spend time in trees, where their thin bodies blend in with branches and afford them protection from predators or overeager herpetologists.

Racers have a generalist diet to go with their name, and the species in our area have been documented eating birds, bats, frogs, lizards, other snakes, and a variety of insects. These snakes hunt using their great speed and exceptional eyesight; they are not considered venomous but rather catch and subdue prey with their powerful jaws. They can be difficult to handle and are wont to bite; though not venomous, the bite might not be pleasant, so handle with care. Racers and whipsnakes all lay eggs in mid-summer (June/July), from a handful up to 30 per clutch. To see a racer or a whipsnake, we suggest hiking on cleared trails in the mid-mornings or late afternoons. The more time spent on the trails, the more likely you are to catch a glimpse of one before it rockets away.

The Alameda whipsnake (a subspecies of California whipsnake) is threatened by urbanization.

Coachwhips come in many flavors; this morph is commonly known as a red racer.

## A BRIEF TOUR OF OUR SPECIES AND SUBSPECIES

In our area we have two subspecies of the common racer, a widespread species found across the United States. The western yellow-bellied racer occurs in northern and coastal California, Oregon, eastern Washington, northern Nevada and Utah, and southern Idaho. The eastern yellow-bellied racer occurs only across Montana in our region. Juveniles have dark blotches on a pale background; adults usually have plain-colored backs and the namesake yellow belly. These racers can be found in open meadows, prairies, and forest clearings.

The most common and well-known whipsnake is the coachwhip. It ranges from central California and Nevada down through Arizona and New Mexico, as well as east of the Continental Divide. The coachwhip has lots of color variation; some individuals are a bubblegum pink, but others can be a more muted gray or tan. Their tolerance for high temperatures and dry areas allows them to be active during the day and maintain a wide range of habitats, from deserts to forested areas. Coachwhips can be feisty and may attempt to strike anyone who gets too close.

Another coach-whip pokes its head through the desert scrub.

The California whipsnake occurs across much of the state, excluding the Central Valley, and extends down to Baja. It has a darker body than other whipsnakes and a prominent light stripe on either side of body. The color lightens toward the tail, and the underside is a light cream, pink, or yellow. This snake prefers chaparral and scrub habitats where it can hunt during the day. One subspecies, the Alameda whipsnake, is found only in the Bay Area. It can be distinguished by wide orange stripes on the side.

Other whipsnakes include the striped whipsnake, which is characterized by alternating dark and light longitudinal stripes. It often has a pink or red tail below. This species can be found in every state in our region. It frequents a variety of habitats but is partial to rocky outcroppings, including those in stream beds and grasslands.

The Sonoran whipsnake is found only in Arizona and extreme southwestern New Mexico. The head and neck are often a dark gray-green, fading to a light green or tan at the tail. It may have light spots but lacks the crisp stripes of the striped whipsnake. This snake is highly arboreal and terrestrial; look for it across mountain slopes in desert scrub, woodland, and grassland regions.

# variable groundsnake

*Sonora semiannulata*

**FUN FACT**

"Variable" indeed: it can be banded, striped, or solid in color.

| SIZE | FOOD | SPECIES IN OUR AREA |
| --- | --- | --- |
| 8–20 inches | lizards, scorpions, spiders, crickets | 1 |

The variable groundsnake is a relatively small, nocturnal, and secretive semi-fossorial species that lives in dry rocky and sandy areas in a variety of ecosystems including grasslands, chaparral, and woodland from sea level up to 5,000 feet. Despite its small size, the species' range is huge, and it can be found in most western and southwestern states, from Idaho, Oregon, and California, across to Texas and Missouri, as well as throughout northeastern Mexico and in Baja.

The variable groundsnake comes in several colors; here is the striped morph.

Overall coloration and pattern can vary across the range and might cause different individuals to appear to be totally separate species. Some individuals bear a coral snake–like pattern with incomplete black bands that do not circle the entire orange/red body. The number of these bands can vary. In other regions, they can be evenly brown or have an even orange-tan along the entire dorsal part of the body, with light brown sides. Some individuals can have a black neck band, and generally, underparts are gray or white, which helps to separate them from black-necked snakes, which have orange bellies. Head is round and has no "neck"—the head is pretty much as thick and cylindrical as the rest of the body. Most individuals reach maturity after two years, and females lay four to six eggs during summer.

Groundsnakes like rocky areas with loose soil for burrowing.

## A "RARE" COMMON SPECIES

Variable groundsnakes are thought to be common in many areas; however, they are hard to spot because of their secretive behavior. They can be active during the day but more likely will be under some kind of cover—rocks, vegetation clumps, and, of course, our old favorite, plywood sheets. During warm nights and especially after rain, they will venture to the surface. That's why your best chance to see them is during night walks along steep and rocky outcrops, or car cruising slow enough that you will be able to spot their little bodies. They are often found in backyards, even in metropolitan areas like Phoenix and Tucson.

## MIDPOINT IN THE FOOD CHAIN

The diet of groundsnakes consists of a variety of small lizards and arthropods, including scorpions, centipedes, crickets, insect larvae, and spiders. Slotted rear teeth indicate that they might produce some type of mild venom to help paralyze or digest their prey, but it does not represent a danger for humans. Additionally, this species is known to be very calm and, if picked up, usually does not try to bite. Yet that which eats faces the prospect of being eaten itself. Variable groundsnakes are part of the diet of many other larger animals, including birds and coral snakes, and there is even a record of a large centipede eating a small individual.

# gopher snake

***Pituophis catenifer***

**FUN FACT**

This variable species sometimes hibernates with other snakes.

| SIZE | FOOD | SPECIES IN OUR AREA |
| --- | --- | --- |
| 1.5–8 feet | rodents, rabbits, birds, lizards | 1 |

With any animal, from the biggest bear to the longest snake, size can be hard to certify. Everybody wants to say their catch is the largest, heaviest, strangest, tallest, or most "-est" of all. Claims are too rarely backed up with verified data. Even so, with some individuals over 7 feet long, gopher snakes are almost certainly the largest snakes in our area. Of course, most individuals won't challenge the record books, and on average, gopher snakes are 2–5 feet long. Still, this is usually a reasonably big snake. Individuals are sexually mature once they reach about 2 feet long.

A good example of a generalist, the gopher snake occurs in a variety of environments, including grasslands, woodlands, piñon-juniper forest, and even farmlands, from 2,000 to 9,500 feet. The range includes most of the western United States (excepting the highest parts of the Rocky Mountains and extreme northwestern Washington State) and the northern third of Mexico. With that much territory, names are likely to vary from region to region; subspecies range from Churchill's bullsnake to blow snake to Sonoran gopher snake.

Basic color is a tan or yellow base coat, a small black line across the cheek and eye, and another below the eye, and red, black, or brown stripes, diamonds, or splotches along the back.

[left] Different subspecies of gopher snakes can exhibit different color patterns and reach a range of sizes. This is a Sonoran gopher snake.

[opposite, top] Gopher snakes inhabit almost any habitat type you can imagine, and several subspecies exist.

[opposite, bottom] Famous for having "personality"—some gopher snakes can be really tame; others are very defensive and will hiss or strike if approached.

## GOOD NEIGHBORS

In general, these primarily ground-dwelling snakes eat small mammals, occasionally birds and reptiles. They are often found in rocky areas where rodents are abundant. Gopher snakes kill their prey by constriction and are important rodent control agents in the ecosystem, helping reduce outbreaks of diseases like hantavirus by controlling their vector species. In turn, they themselves are part of the natural cycle and can be eaten by hawks and eagles.

## IMPRESSIVE DISPLAY

Because they can hiss and be aggressive, gopher snakes are sometimes confused with rattlesnakes. You can easily tell the difference because this species lacks the keratinized "rattles" at the tip of the tail; they will also most likely be longer and slimmer than most rattlesnakes. Yet most deserve an award for playing the part well (would a snake Oscar be called a Herpy?), and the defensive behavior can consist of flattening the head, puffing the body, and

coiling, all while producing a loud hissing—mimicking a rattlesnake so well, it even vibrates the tip of the tail. If there are dried leaves or grass stems, this generates a convincing, buzzing rattle. All this high drama is not a bluff: they *will* strike. They may lack venom, but bites can be painful and can lead to infections if the wound is not cleaned thoroughly and swiftly. If a cranky gopher snake is doing the rattlesnake dance at you, the what-to-do-next part is simple: back off and give it space.

Nature is predictable and orderly, except when it isn't, and the senior author fondly remembers Reginald and Llewellyn, a two-headed gopher snake that lived over a decade at the Los Angeles Zoo in the 1970s and '80s.

# glossy snake

## *Arizona elegans*

**FUN FACT**

Common name and specific epithet refer to this snake's smooth dorsal scales.

| SIZE | FOOD | SPECIES IN OUR AREA |
| --- | --- | --- |
| 1–5.5 feet | lizards, other snakes, small mammals | 1 |

A glossy snake looks like a slimmed-down gopher snake.

This snake ranges across the southern portion of the American West, from central to Southern California and across to Texas, and into northern Mexico (and of course, as the eponymous genus name suggests, throughout most of Arizona). Of medium length, this snake is on the slender side—yes, with experience, one can tell a stout snake from one that is a bit more svelte—with a cream or gray base color and brown blotches along the back.

Active at night, this snake is commonly found while driving slowly down quiet roads on warm, summer evenings. During the day it spends time underground. It can be found in desert scrub habitat and grasslands, where loose soils and sands accommodate burrowing. In the winter it hibernates underground.

Smooth scales distinguish this snake from the similar-looking gopher snake. The glossy snake also has a countersunk lower jaw, which gives it the appearance of having a severe overbite. Lizards, other snakes, and small mammals keep this snake full and happy. It subdues prey with constriction when needed but will often down sleeping lizards when they can be found. The slim build and glossy scales of this snake should readily separate it from rattlesnakes, but the glossy snake doesn't want you to know that. When threatened, it may rattle its tail, mimicking the rattle of its venomous neighbors. This snake is not venomous, though, and is usually docile when handled.

[above] A snake's tongue can convey many data points, including changes in temperature.

[below] Right habitat, but somebody please turn off the lights: look for the glossy snake in desert like this, but only after dark.

# kingsnakes

## *Lampropeltis* spp.

**FUN FACT**

Several species of kingsnakes mimic venomous coral snakes.

| SIZE | FOOD | SPECIES IN OUR AREA |
|---|---|---|
| 2–5 feet | other snakes, small mammals, reptiles, birds, eggs | 9: gray-banded kingsnake (*L. alterna*), California kingsnake (*L. californiae*), common kingsnake (*L. getula*), Sonoran mountain kingsnake (*L. knoblochi*), coast mountain kingsnake (*L. multifasciata*), mountain kingsnake (*L. pyromelana*), desert kingsnake (*L. splendida*), milk snake (*L. triangulum*), California mountain kingsnake (*L. zonata*) |

Kingsnakes are medium-sized, mostly ground-dwelling constrictors found at low to mid-elevations. All species belong to the genus *Lampropeltis* ("shiny shields"), a reference to the sheen of their scales. In the western United States, they range from southern Oregon and some parts in southwestern Montana south through Southern California, Arizona, New Mexico, and Texas and on into northern Mexico, with species diversity increasing as one heads south. These snakes are mostly nocturnal and kill their prey by constriction. Some specialize in eating other snakes; in fact, common kingsnakes are immune to the venom of some vipers and can even prey on rattlesnakes.

California kingsnakes typically are black and white just like this one, but some color morphs can be black and yellow, or can sport brick red and bright white.

Sonoran mountain kingsnakes are among the most beautiful snakes in North America.

Kingsnakes are found in a large variety of habitats, from pine forest to lowland deserts. Recent studies have found that kingsnakes are able to produce the strongest constriction, pound per pound, of any comparable snake, thanks to their muscle configuration and because their tissue is able to function with less oxygen than typical.

**Desert kingsnakes eat mice, lizards, and even small rattlesnakes.**

## COLORFUL WARNING COLORS: TRUTH IN ADVERTISING?

Usually bold colors warn others, "Venomous: Stay Away." That's not true here. (But again, never touch a snake, please, without being *completely* sure what it is.) Many species of kingsnakes mimic the coloration of the venomous coral snakes. Rings of bright yellow-white, red-orange, and black-gray banding offer kingsnakes the appearance of real coral snakes and help deter potential predators. This strategy, Batesian mimicry, is used by non-venomous animals to look like dangerous ones. In some cases, different populations within the same species can have

This coast mountain kingsnake was formerly considered a subspecies of California mountain kingsnake, which ranges from Washington to Baja.

more than one color pattern. Some of the differences in coloration can be more extreme than others; some morphs have only slight changes in the thickness of the rings in the body, whereas you can find others with completely different patterns. The gray-banded kingsnake and common kingsnake are excellent examples of this.

## HOW MANY SPECIES?

Over the years, species with wide-ranging distributions have been recognized to have several subspecies based on differences in morphology, color patterns, and even behavior. Kingsnakes are more diverse in the Southwest, and in recent years several of these subspecies have been recognized as full species. Our listing here shows current consensus, but some authorities look at the same pie and divide it into larger or smaller pieces.

Are kingsnakes aggressive? Like gopher snakes, if cornered in the wild, they can react strongly and will hiss, bite, and vigorously rattle the tip of the tail. Yet at the same time, kingsnakes tame fairly quickly and can make good pets. We say that last sentence with hesitation: it is better not to collect from wild populations, and if buying pet kingsnakes, please patronize vendors selling only ethically sourced animals.

# Mexican hognose snake

*Heterodon kennerlyi*

FUN FACT

Deserves to win an award for excellent death-feigning displays.

| SIZE | FOOD | SPECIES IN OUR AREA |
| --- | --- | --- |
| 1–2.5 feet | small vertebrates, preferably toads | 1 |

A fan favorite of herpetologists, the Mexican hognose snake has earned a reputation for being quite the drama queen. When approached, this snake will often launch into an elaborate "death feign," a display intended to convince predators—"No, really, I'm dead, don't eat me." The snake will roll onto its back, open its mouth wide, and pop its cloaca: "Really, I'm *dead*." The trick might work on the snake's predators, such as birds of prey and mammals like coyotes and raccoons. But a keen observer might notice that the snake, while pretending to be dead, will check to see if you are still watching and, if necessary, redo the display. "Oh, you didn't believe me before? Well, I'm *really* dead this time."

Another anti-predator defense of this stout creature? Mimicry. Its blotched patterns lend a faint resemblance to some rattlesnakes, and its neck-flattening behavior gives the appearance of a cobra. What the hognose snake probably doesn't realize is that there are no cobras in North America. This snake may also coil its tail tightly and hold it upright, which is another way to distract predators.

## POP! GOES THE TOAD

This snake prefers sandy habitats, where it uses its upturned ("hog") nose to dig and hunt for prey. A favorite snack is toads; when the snake gets ahold of a puffed-up toad, it uses large rear teeth to deflate and consume the animal. Hognose snakes have mild venom that is not necessarily dangerous to humans, but there have been cases of swelling after a bite. Other food items include salamanders, frogs, other snakes, small mammals, and eggs of birds and reptiles.

## SIMILAR SPECIES AND RANGE

You are unlikely to confuse this snake with others in our area: the wide body and upturned nose give it a unique look. At first glance you might think this is a rattlesnake, but dark bands across the face, snout shape, and lack of rattles distinguish it readily. The Mexican hognose snake is found only in southeastern Arizona and

Areas teeming with toads and loose, sandy soil make ideal habitats for hognose snakes.

Hognose snakes can flare their necks to appear cobra-like and larger than they actually are.

southwestern New Mexico. The plains subspecies can be found in eastern New Mexico and north to Canada and Montana on the east side of the Rocky Mountains. Though this snake has a limited range in our area, it's worth the drive to see it.

# ring-necked snake

*Diadophis punctatus*

FUN FACT

Bright colors on the underside and tail vary across its range.

| SIZE | FOOD | SPECIES IN OUR AREA |
| --- | --- | --- |
| 1–2.5 feet | smaller herps, insects | 1 |

This small snake has a very large range from California to the southeastern United States. In our region they can be found in coastal California, Oregon, extreme southwestern Washington, broadly in Arizona and New Mexico, and portions of Nevada and Utah. Many subspecies have been described on the basis of geography and color variation. Despite this, the ring-necked snake is still considered a single species.

Ring-necked snakes have bright colors underneath that they flash to predators.

[above] A closer look at the bright ventral colors and curled tail.

[opposite, top] These snakes like habitats with moist soil.

[opposite, bottom] This individual has a crisp collar, but some lack the "ring neck."

The ring-necked snake can be found in a variety of moist habitats such as meadows, grasslands, and forests. Though it is nocturnal and generally secretive, these snakes tend to be locally abundant where they occur. They can often be found by flipping rocks and logs in suitable habitat.

## TO EAT AND AVOID BEING EATEN

The back is a grayish green, usually but not always with the namesake light collar. Underneath this snake is brightly colored, from red to orange to yellow with variation across its range. When faced with a predator, these snakes will flash their colorful underbellies and curl their tail. Why do they curl their tails? Some scientists think it is to signal predators "I see you!" and even to startle them. Others think it acts as a decoy. If a predator takes a chunk of tail, the snake can still get away. One study found that ring-necked snakes had damaged tails more often than other snakes with similar sizes and ecologies, suggesting the tails do act as a decoy to predators. If you find one, you may notice another of its antipredator defenses: secreting a stinky musk from its cloaca.

Tail colors vary across the range.

It feeds on other snakes, lizards, salamanders, tadpoles, insects, slugs, and worms. Diet is thought to vary across this snake's range. This snake's small size and rear fangs render it harmless to humans, but one study showed that the ring-necked snake's venom is potent enough to kill a garter snake, a species upon which they prey.

# garter snakes

## *Thamnophis* spp.

**FUN FACT**

Some become temporarily poisonous after eating newts.

| SIZE | FOOD | SPECIES IN OUR AREA |
|---|---|---|
| 12–65 inches, depending on species and life stage | amphibians, fish, rodents, slugs | 12: aquatic garter snake (*T. atratus*), Sierra garter snake (*T. couchii*), black-necked garter snake (*T. cyrtopsis*), terrestrial garter snake (*T. elegans*), Mexican garter snake (*T. eques*), two-striped garter snake (*T. hammondii*), checkered garter snake (*T. marcianus*), northwestern garter snake (*T. ordinoides*), western ribbon snake (*T. proximus*), Plains garter snake (*T. radix*), narrow-headed garter snake (*T. rufipunctatus*), common garter snake (*T. sirtalis*) |

Some of our most common and friendly snakes, the garter snakes (often mistakenly referred to as "garden" or "gardener" snakes) inhabit many different environments across the West, and you very well could have one in your garden.

Garter snakes vary in coloration and pattern, but most often can be recognized by a light cream, yellow, or orange line running along the spine, and/or two light lines running along the sides of the body where the back scales meet the ventral scales. The common name comes from the resemblance of these stripes to the around-the-leg straps (garters) that used to hold up men's socks and are still part of bridalwear.

Anywhere you go in our area, you can find one or more garter snake species. Some have large ranges, such as the terrestrial garter snake, which occurs in all western states, or the common garter snake, which occurs broadly across the Pacific Northwest. Others have small ranges, like the Mexican garter snake in

A black-necked garter snake hangs out near a frog pond in the Chiricahua Mountains.

the extreme south of Arizona, the narrow-headed garter snake, restricted to a few localities in central Arizona and western New Mexico, or the northwestern garter snake in coastal Oregon and Washington.

Garter snakes are generally associated with water, though they vary in their affinity for it. The narrow-headed garter snake is almost exclusively found in water, where it uses its sharp, recurved teeth to hunt for fish. The aquatic garter snake is also highly dependent on water, where it eats mostly amphibians. None of the garter snakes are venomous to humans, but some people have reported swelling and bleeding after a bite, probably because garter snakes have anticoagulants in their saliva, which prevents blood from clotting.

## ARMS RACE

Earlier, you read about the toxic newts in the genus *Taricha*. Though many predators have learned to associate their bright orange or red color with danger and avoid them altogether, some garter snakes have another trick: evolving resistance to the newt's toxins. A famous tall tale that has spread around herpetologist circles for years is that of a group of hunters, found dead unexpectedly at their campsite with no signs of injury or foul play. Upon further inspection, a rough-skinned newt was found in their coffee pot—if one newt can kill several adult humans, how does a garter snake stand a chance?

**All snakes gather information with their tongues, collecting scent molecules in the air.**

Newts carry tetrodotoxin, a toxin also found in deadly pufferfish, that prevents sodium ion channels from working properly (sodium ion channels are what allows your muscles to contract and nerves to fire). But these snakes have specially shaped ion channels that prevent tetrodotoxin from interfering. Even more interesting, evolutionary biologists have shown that some of the mutations underlying the unique channel shape in garter snakes

Wandering garter snakes (a subspecies of terrestrial garter snake) are found in a variety of habitats, hence their common name.

Narrow-headed garter snakes use their long rows of razor-sharp teeth to snag fish out of the water.

are actually older than the snakes themselves: they were predisposed to be resistant.

So what happens when a garter snake eats a toxic newt? The snake may then become temporarily poisonous (not venomous) to predators by retaining the tetrodotoxin. Research has shown that as newts get more poisonous, the snakes become more resistant. Newts themselves are only resistant to tetrodotoxin, not immune, so there is a limit to how toxic they can become. And garter snakes injected with the toxin are still affected—they may slow down, or become temporarily paralyzed, but most will recover quickly after sequestering the toxins. Only time will tell who will win this arms race.

Garter snakes are good swimmers and may take to the water in search of frogs or fish.

Garter snakes enjoy other foods, including other amphibians, fish, rodents, and banana slugs for some specialists like the northwestern garter snake. Many species in colder areas hibernate communally in dens, sometimes with hundreds of other snakes. In the spring, males leave the hibernaculum to warm up and prepare to find mates. When the females emerge, they emit chemical signals that males pick up on. Many males then compete to mate with the receptive female, forming a mating ball and fighting for her attention. The winning snake mates with the female, who will then give birth to live young in the late summer.

# WEBSITES AND FURTHER READING

## Websites

AmphibiaWeb / amphibiaweb.org

California Herps / californiaherps.com

HerpMapper / herpmapper.org

iNaturalist / inaturalist.org

Reptiles and Amphibians of Arizona / reptilesofaz.org

Reptile Database / reptile-database.org

## Books

Bezy, Robert. 2019. *Night Lizards: Field Memoirs and a Summary of the Xantusiidae*. ECO.

Brennan, Thomas, and Andrew Holycross. 2006. *Amphibians and Reptiles in Arizona*. Arizona Game and Fish Department.

Crump, Marty. 2011. *Amphibians and Reptiles: An Introduction to Their Natural History and Conservation*. McDonald & Woodward.

Degenhardt, William, Charles Painter, and Andrew Price. 1996. *Amphibians and Reptiles of New Mexico*. University of New Mexico Press.

Holycross, Andrew, and Joseph Mitchell. 2020. *Snakes of Arizona*. ECO.

Jones, Lawrence, and Rob Lovich. 2009. *Lizards of the American Southwest: A Photographic Field Guide*. Rio Nuevo Publishers.

Jones, Lawrence, William Leonard, and Deanna H. Olson. 2016. *Amphibians of the Pacific Northwest*. Seattle Audubon Society.

Petty, Micha, Andrew Durso, and Sabina Squires. 2019. *A Primer on Reptiles and Amphibians*. Louisiana Exotic Animal Resource Network.

Rubio, Manny. 1998. *Rattlesnake: Portrait of a Predator*. Smithsonian Institution Press.

Stebbins, Robert. 2003. *A Field Guide to Western Reptiles and Amphibians*, 3rd ed. Houghton Mifflin.

Stebbins, Robert, and Samuel McGinnis. 2012. *Field Guide to Amphibians and Reptiles of California*, rev. ed. University of California Press.

St. John, Alan. 2002. *Reptiles of the Northwest: Alaska to California; Rockies to the Coast*. Lone Pine Publishing.

# PHOTO CREDITS

Fred Hood, pages 32 (top), 85, 90, 112, 114, 185, 198.

Charles R. Peterson, pages 61, 62.

Kurt van Wyk, page 65.

Gary Nafis, page 81.

Paul Carter, pages 97, 206, 207.

Jarrod Swackhamer, page 113.

Francesca Heras, page 197 (top).

R. C. Clark / Dancing Snake Nature Photography, page 197 (bottom).

*All other photos are by the authors.*

# INDEX

## a

# b



# c

## d



## e

# f



# g

# h



# i

## m



## n

# O



# P

# r

# S

# U



# V



# W

## X



## Y



## Z

# ABOUT THE AUTHORS

JOSÉ GABRIEL MARTÍNEZ-FONSECA

JOSÉ GABRIEL MARTÍNEZ-FONSECA

**Charles Hood** grew up by the Los Angeles River, where at the age of 10 he saw his first snake. He has been a Fulbright scholar, an Artist-in-Residence with the National Science Foundation, and a Research Fellow with the Nevada Museum of Art's Center for Art + Environment. In his travels he has eaten mopani worms in Zambia and live ants in the Amazon; he has also been to the South Pole and part way to the North Pole. Charles worked on Timber's *Wild LA*, and he also has published fiction, essays on art, and two other nature guides: one on birds and one on mammals. He lives in the Mojave Desert and always has extra water in his car and at least one snake hook, just to help scoot things off midnight roads.

Born in the San Francisco Bay Area, biologist **Erin Westeen** became fascinated with herps at a young age: her first encounters were western fence lizards, which she would observe and catch in her yard. She has done extensive fieldwork across western North America and in the Neotropics, and every trip, no matter how far from home, turns into a quest to find and document local species. Currently she is a Ph.D. candidate at UC Berkeley, where she studies trait evolution and speciation in spiny lizards. When not in the field, you can find her in one of the many natural history museums in which she has been lucky enough to work.

ERIN WESTEEN

**José Gabriel Martínez-Fonseca** is a Nicaraguan biologist and wildlife photographer who has been working with amphibians, reptiles, and mammals (especially bats) for over 12 years. Fascinated by snakes long before he caught his first one at the age of 11, he later co-authored a *Field Guide to the Amphibians and Reptiles of Nicaragua*. Over the years, José has added several new species to Nicaragua's herp and mammal checklists and has expanded knowledge of faunal distributions in Central America. Currently he is a Ph.D. student at Northern Arizona University, studying how habitat fragmentation in the Neotropics affects wildlife. He has been enjoying the opportunity to use his time in the Southwest to find and photograph as many species of amphibians and reptiles as possible.